The Wedding's Over. . .

What Now?

by
Eddie Lewis

QUALITY PUBLICATIONS
P.O. BOX 1060
ABILENE, TEXAS 79604-1060
(915) 677-6262

ISBN: 0-89137-574-0

This book is DEDICATED TO:

My Mother—Mary W. Lewis, for guiding my feet
    on a path to a happy life.

My Wife—Judy, who has helped me grow in love
    and know the joy of giving myself.

My two Daughters—Angelia and Christy, who have
    helped me experience the joy of
    fatherhood.

Foreword

The Wedding's Over. . .What Now? is a practical book by a caring author. It grew out of seminars on the family conducted principally in Mississippi/Arkansas by Eddie and Judy Lewis.

This kind of book was in such short supply only a generation ago. Many of us could have strengthened relationships, become better role models, and lived with fewer regrets if we had been introduced to such an empathetic study early in our marriages.

Eddie Lewis has relied on some of the most popular authors of family studies in America today for statistics, illustrations and observations. He has set these in his own framework of Biblical study and ministerial experience. The result is a thoughtful treatment of the various relationships of family life, accompanied by questions to stimulate discussion and instruments for self-evaluation.

I have known Eddie for well over a decade and have had some opportunity to observe him as a student and as a minister. It is refreshing to see this sensitive, Biblical examination of the principles of Christian family life flow from his life and ministry.

Harold Hazelip

Introduction

For a number of years Judy and I have conducted our "Family Enrichment Seminar." We feel the seminar has been a great help to every congregation that has hosted it. This book is a result of the material we have used in these seminars to help families grow in their love and understanding of each other.

I don't claim to have all the answers about how to raise children, or be the best husband on earth. I do know that love, communication, understanding, consideration, and giving of yourself to your spouse and family are necessary if you are to succeed in being the husband and father God wants you to be. That is my goal and I know that many of you want the same thing.

In this book I have set forth some goals for husbands and wives. I realize that no one can live up to every statement, but the great truth is, we don't have to. If we have a DESIRE to do our best, and WORK at succeeding in these areas; if we do our best to make the needed changes in our lives, we will be good husbands and wives.

God has not promised us that Christian marriages will never have problems. Any marriage can have problems! But the great thing about a Christian marriage is that if both partners will practice their Christianity the marriage can blossom into a beautiful relationship. If you have problems in your marriage realize that working them out, no matter what the problem is, can be done. And that saving that marriage will ultimately draw you closer to each other as you discuss and work at truly solving the problems.

Marriage is great! I can't imagine being single. Judy is a intrical part of my life. I know that our relationship has grown over the years. We are still learning new things about how we feel. Changes occur every day, as we grow older, that effect our relationship. But we change together. She understands me and I try to understand her. She does a better job at this than I do. But I try, and as a result we grow closer everyday and more in love. The same thing can happen to you in your marriage. All it takes is love, and time, and a willingness to give of yourself to the most important person in your life.

I encourage you to read this book no matter what your age, or how many years you have been married. The questions and tests can be used as a spring board to greater and deeper understanding of each other.

I appreciate your desire to grow in your marriage.

Love,
Eddie

Table of Contents

PART I: Husband/Wife Relations
CHAPTER 1
God's Design For Marriage

A happy home and marriage have been part of the conversation of Christians throughout the ages. We ask: "What makes a marriage happy?"; "What is a good husband?"; "What is a good wife?"; "What makes a home a happy place?" I hope to answer some of these questions from my experience as a husband and father, and the insights I have gained through my study and God's word.

We can see the need for such a study by considering some statistics. The divorce rate is one in two. That means for every divorce granted in the United States last year, there were two marriages performed.

A more meaningful statistic, to the state of marriage, is the average length of a marriage is six years.[1] How many have been married twenty years? For every marriage of twenty years there are two or three that lasted less than a year. How many have been married for fifty years? For every marriage of fifty years there are eight marriages that have lasted less than a year. To me it is heart breaking to see so many unsuccessful marriages.

Another statistic that hurts is five of every six marriages are broken in heart.[2] Eighty-three percent of the marriages that are still together are unhappy. Only seventeen percent of the marriages in our land are happy. How sad!

The church is not excluded! The "Herald of Truth" program reports that they receive the most response from programs that deal with the "family" or "marriage", and that most of their responses are from members of the church.[3]

1

What does that say? We need to deal more with this unique relationship. As our families go, so goes the church.

Definitions Of Marriage

To give a scriptural basis to this study, consider some of the definitions given for marriage.

1. **CIVIL AGREEMENT.** Some say it is a civil agreement only. A man and a woman agree to live together as hsband and wife and to share common property. This is not all there is to marriage because God has given some requirements for the marriage relationship.

"What God has joined together, let man not separate." Matthew 19:6b.

"For the woman who has a husband is bound by the law to her husband as long as he lives. But if the husband dies, she is released from the law of the husband." Romans 7:2.[4]

These statements are only a few of the requirements God has placed on the marriage. So it is far more than just a civil agreement.

2. **INSTITUTION OF THE CHURCH.** Some feel it is an institution of the church and should be regulated by the church. This is not true because marriage existed before the church. It is true that in the New Testament some teachings are given that help regulate the marriage, but marriage is not an institution of the church.

3. **MADE IN HEAVEN.** I believe the best way to describe marriage is to say they are made in heaven. God has given all the laws, rules, and regulations that should govern the marriage and that make a marriage a success. Therefore, we have to recognize Him as the source for happy, successful marriages. Marriages are made in heaven, but as someone said, "the maintenace work is done on earth."

The definition of marriage, I believe, that agrees with scripture is: "A Covenant Establishing a Home." It is a covenant between a man and a woman to establish and develop a home. A *covenant* is more than an agreement, although most would define it that way. It carries the idea of a promise, a binding, a welding together of the people involved, so that there is no thought of divorce.

God has given only one reason one may dissolve a marriage, Matthew 19. But, it was not so from the beginning. God's thought was to join one man to one woman for one lifetime. Mark 10:1-9. Even when Moses made other exceptions God was not pleased. When God joins them, He doesn't want them to separate.

God took the rib from Adam's side and made the woman. She was to be a "helper, suitable" for man. Adam said after her creation, "This is now bone of my bones, and flesh of my flesh; she shall be called 'Woman', because she was taken out of Man. Therefore (for this

2

reason of marriage, to establish a home) a man will leave his father and mother and be united to his wife, and they will become one flesh." Genesis 2:23,24. Other scriptures support this passage, Matthew 19:5-6, Ephesians 5:31.

Marriage is a covenant establishing a home. It is not just to have *children,* though that is a primary reason for marriage. God told Adam and Eve, "Be fruitful and multiply; fill the earth and subdue it." Genesis 1:28. This purpose is not the main reason for marriage. It is to establish a home.

Marriage is not just for *companionship,* though this too is a primary reason. God said, "It is not good for the man to be alone; I will make a helper comparable to him." Genesis 2:18. It is natural for man to desire the companionship of a woman. God created us that way! Other verses indicate the importance of this relationship. But again, this is not the main reason for marriage. It is to establish a home.

Marriage is not just to *satisfy the natural desire for sex,* though this too is a primary reason. Proverbs 5:19 plainly states that marriage is to provide a lawful outlet for these desires. Paul says, "Marriage is honorable among all, and the bed undefiled; but fornicators. . .God will judge." Hebrews 13:4.

> *"Let each man have his own wife, and let each woman have her own husband. Let the husband render to his wife the affection due her, and likewise also the wife to her husband. The wife does not have authority over her own body, but the husband does. And likewise the husband does not have authority over his own body, but the wife does. Do not deprive one another except with consent. . .then come together again so that Satan does not tempt you."* 1 Corinthians 7:2-5.

Passion is not a dirty word. It describes the natural desire for sex that God has given to every man and woman. The only time it becomes dirty or wrong is when it is satisfied in some unholy way. Sex is an important part of a successful marriage.

All these reasons play a part in marriage. They each have a part in making up the complete relationship. But the major reason for marriage is still, "A Covenant to Establish a Home."

Priorities In Marriage

With this definition in mind, consider some priorities in marriage. I believe we have the problems we face in marriage today because we have our priorities all mixed up. What is important to most people is the wrong things.

Using Ephesians chapters 5 and 6 as the outline for these priorities, consider *five main priorities* for the Christian marriage.

3

1. **DAILY WALKS WITH GOD.** "Be followers of God as dear children. . .For you were once darkness, but now you are light in the Lord. Walk as children of light. . ." Ephesians 5:1,8. This walk should consume our time and energy daily. "Whatever you do, in word or deed, do all in the name of the Lord Jesus. . ." Colossians 3:17. We are to daily live for Jesus. We are to grow in our relationship with Him. Husbands and wives are to grow individually and together in Jesus Christ.

Daniel, in the Old Testament, didn't let anything interfere with his daily devotion to God. Even when the King made a decree to stop all prayers in the land except to the King, Daniel would not stop his daily prayer. Three times each day he faced Jerusalem and prayed to God, and God protected Daniel as a result. Daniel 6:10,22. Even when he was thrown into the lion's den.

Jesus commands us, "But seek first the kingdom of God and His righteousness, and all these things shall be added to you." Matthew 6:33. We have to seek God first. God and our personal relationship to Him has to be number one in our marriage.

2. **OUR SPOUSE.** Beginning with verse 22, Paul considers the family relationships. He starts with the husband and wife. This relationship has to be the most important, even above our children and parents. Why? Because these two have been joined by God, and everyone else was added after this initial joining. When your parents are gone, either by death or moving away, and the children have grown up and started their own families, you and your spouse will be together all by yourselves. You need to have a good relationship before that time comes.

The wife is to submit to her husband as the church submits to Christ. Verses 22,23. She respects his work as a leader of the family, and supports him in this role in every way. Verse 33.

The husband is to *love* his wife as Christ loved the church and died for it. Verse 25. Paul describes this love, which is *APAGE* (the Greek word for unconditional love), by saying he loves her as he loves his own body and feeds and cares for it. Verse 29.

What a beautiful relationship described here by Paul of a husband and a wife. It is the most important human relationship we can have.

3. **OUR CHILDREN.** In chapter 6 Paul mentions the next most important relationship or priority - our children. Paul says to the *children*, "Obey your parents in the Lord, for this is right. 'Honor thy father and mother'. . .that it may be well with you and you may live long on the earth." Verses 1-3.

Paul says to the *father*, "Do not provoke your children to wrath, but bring them up in the training and admonition of the Lord." Verse 4.

4

The parents are responsible to teach or train their children to love God, and live a life for Him. Many parents don't see the need to teach or train, nor realize that everything they do is part of the training their children receive about how to live a Christian life.

In Deuteronomy 6:4-9, Moses tells the Israelites to teach their children. The method is to write the commands of God on the door post, on their bracelet, talk to them as you walk together, or sit down, or play together. In all of life's situations teaching is done and the parent is responsible for what is taught.

It is sad that many parents disregard this important responsibility and let T.V., music, and friends do the teaching of their children. One person said, "Family devotionals in an otherwise pagan home do no good!" I agree! Our homes have to be Christian in every way. Having a devotional once in a while will not make your home Christian, if fighting, bad attitudes, non-involvement with Christ, prevail in that home. Our children have got to see positive Christian action on our part.

Communication is a key in teaching our children. The average time of communicating between parent and child is about seventeen minutes a day. Researchers say sixteen of those minutes are used in giving commands or instruction about what they are to do, so only one minute a day is used in real communication. Mrs. Laura Cole said, "You can't fuss at your child all the time and expect him to love you back!" I agree! They need to know and feel a parent's love.

Many fathers neglect their children. Not by lack of material possessions, or lack of food and shelter, but by *time*. They fill their lives with activities so that nothing is left for the child or wife. If we neglect our children they will strike back, and usually it is at the thing that has required all our time. Think about it! I devote an entire chapter in this book to communication because it is so important in our relationship within the family.

Here are four suggestions to help improve our communication with our children: - Have an open display of affection for that child. I love to see a father play with his child. To see that big hairy arm reach out and grab the child as he runs by. To see him kiss the child, or tickle the child. What a great way to show love!

- Mutual family support. The family supports every other family member in activities that the child, or the father, or the mother participates. We support each other!

- Family rituals. Some unique activity that your family does that is a special time for all to be together, and you let nothing interfere. For example: birthdays, meal time, prayer times, half birthdays, special outing, etc.

- Decisive living. Plan to make things happen in your family. Some feel that others succeed in their family relations naturally, but that is not true. Every successful family is that way because the parents have worked at it and planned for it to succeed.[5]

4. **OUR VOCATION OR JOB.** The fourth priority is our job. In chapter 6 of Ephesians, Paul discusses the working relationship of a slave to his master. I believe Paul gives some good advice about how to deal with our job. To the worker he says, obey, respect, and fear your boss with a sincere heart. Do your work whether the boss is watching or not. When you work, realize that it is not an earthly boss you are serving, but God. You work to bring glory to your heavenly father and God will reward you for the good you do. What a different view Paul gives to the work ethic.

The boss is instructed to treat his employees in the same way and not to threaten them because he has a boss in heaven. Everyone is under the direction of someone else, even the boss.

What a tremendous teaching. We can be a servant of God even on the job. The work we do and our relationship with our fellow workers, or employees, can glorify God if we choose to do that. You don't have to leave your job and work full time for the church to be a fruitful worker in the kingdom. Do your work to the glory of God and He will be pleased with you.

5. **MINISTRY BEYOND OUR DAILY WALK WITH GOD.** Finally, *church work* needs to come after our daily walk with God and our family. You may be surprised that I place it last on my list, but I feel the New Testament places it there. As a husband and father, I have a responsibility to my family to teach them and provide for them. If I convert the world and lose my family to the devil, I have failed in my work as a Christian husband and father.

The church today is to blame for the failure of some husbands because of the time and work it requires of them. As a preacher, I know the hours some preachers put into their ministry. The same is true of elders, deacons, teachers, and other interested workers in the church. But we have got to develop a balance between our work and family needs.

I believe we have a false concept of church work. We view the father as leaving home to go out and do the work of the church. I view the father taking his wife and the children with him as they do the work of the church. By the participation of the wife and children they learn to serve God too. It is a whole family concept.

To promote family togetherness, the local congregations can do a lot to help the family. One, have family gatherings, not adults only, not teens only, but for everyone. Second, have workshops and seminars on family relations. Third, look at films on the family. There are many good films or videos available. Fourth, study in Bible classes about husbands and wives, or family problems. I believe in teaching to prevent problems, not waiting until they come and trying to fix them. Five, promote times for the family to be together for study and recreation.

Conclusion

I hope you will consider the list of priorities and incorporate them into your life. I believe they will make the difference in your marriage. Esther Toland says of "Marriage":

> It's not a lot of beauty
> Nor bright and shining dome,
> Nor satin cushions, silken drapes,
> That help to make a home.

> 'Tis the grace in oneness living,
> The smile, the helping hand,
> The little turns, the thoughtful giving,
> That help a home to stand.

It is oneness living, the smile, the helping hand, the little things you do, the giving, that make a home and a marriage a lasting thing.

A group of ministers and marriage counselors in Lubbock, Texas gave these suggestions about successful marriage.[6]

1). Don't marry in a hurry.
2). Solve your differences before marriage, not after.
3). Avoid a non-realistic concept of love - but have the Christian love of AGAPE. (Unconditional love).
4). Be emotionally mature to accept the responsibility of marriage.
5). Cultivate the "Our" attitude.
6). Develop unity in the family - be loyal to each other even above your parents.
7). View finances soberly.
8). Have a common religion.
9). Make sure you are correctly informed about sex.
10). Marriage is a growing process.

Marriage is the greatest and most precious possession we can have. "Marriage is honorable among all. . ." Hebrews 13:4. It is up to you to make it a success!

Questions

1. Give a Bible definition for marriage. Give your own definition for marriage.

7

2. In the list of priorities for marriage, why do you feel it is important to put the spouse first?

3. Parents can interfere with a couple's relationship. What are some things you can do to help your parents know that your relationship to your mate is number one in importance?

4. Children don't always help a marriage. When should you have children and how do you prepare for their arrival?

5. Is the job more important than the family?

6. What advice would you give to a young couple about to marry about setting priorities?

---

[1]Almanac, 1985.

[2]*Ibid.*

[3]Herald of Truth Programs, Produced by the Highland Church of Christ, Abilene, Texas, 79604.

[4]**The Holy Bible: New King James Version.** Nashville, Tennessee: Thomas Nelson Publishers, 1982. (All Bible references will be made from the NKJV, unless otherwise stated.)

[5]Clifton Rogers, "The Happy Christian Home." A paper presented at the Harding College Lectureship.

[6]Mid McKnight, *Vestibules of Heaven,* Abilene, Texas: McKnight Publications.

"Marriage Questionnaire"

Answer *Yes* or *No* to each question, then check your score below:

1. Do you make your spouse feel good about him or herself? Yes___No___

2. Do you value the same things in your spouse that you value in yourself? Yes___No___

3. Does your face spontaneously break into a smile when you see your spouse? Yes___No___

4. When you leave the house does your spouse have a sense of well-being, having been nourished by your company? Yes___No___

5. Can you and your spouse tell each other honestly what you really want without using manipulation or games? Yes___No___

6. Can your spouse get angry at you without you thinking less of him/her? Yes___No___

7. Can you accept your spouse as he/she is without having plans to redo him/her? Yes___No___

8. Is your behavior consistent with your words? Yes___No___

9. Do your actions really show that you care? Yes___No___

10. Do you enjoy introducing your spouse to your friends and acquaintances? Yes___No___

11. Are you able to share with your spouse your moments of weakness, failure, or disappointments? Yes___No___

12. Would your spouse say you are a good listener? Yes___No___

13. Do you trust your spouse to solve his/her own problems? Yes___No___

14. Do you admit to your spouse that you have problems and need comfort? Yes___No___

15. Do you believe you could live a full and happy life without your spouse? Yes___No___

16. Do you encourage your spouse to develop his/her full potential? Yes___No___

17. Are you able to learn from your spouse and value his/her advice? Yes___No___

18. If your spouse were to die tomorrow, would you be very happy you had had a chance to meet and marry him/her? Yes___No___

19. Does your spouse feel he/she is the most important thing or person in your life? Yes___No___

20. Do you feel you know at least five of your spouse's major needs and how to meet those needs in a skillful way? Yes___No___

21. Do you know what your spouse needs when he/she is under stress and/or is discouraged? Yes___No___

22. When you offend your spouse, do you usually admit you were wrong and seek forgiveness? Yes___No___

23. Would your spouse say you praise him/her at least once a day? Yes___No___

24. Would your spouse say you are open to his/her correction? Yes___No___

25. Would your spouse say you usually consider his/her feelings and ideas when a major decision that affects the family is being made? Yes___No___

26. Would your spouse say you enjoy being with him/her and sharing many of life's experiences? Yes___No___

27. Would your spouse say you are a good example of what you would like him/her to be? Yes___No___

28. Would you say you create interest in your spouse when you share things you consider important? Yes___No___

If you answered "Yes" to 10 or less questions, then your relationship is in major need of overhaul.

If you answered "Yes" to 11-19 of the questions, your relationship is in need of overhaul.

If you answered "Yes" to 20 or more, then you're probably on your way to a good, lasting relationship.

(Used by permission from the book: **If Only He Knew** by Gary Smalley with Steve Scott. Copyright 1979 by Gary T. Smalley, Revised edition copyright 1982 by The Zondervan Corporation.)

CHAPTER 2

The Christian Wife

Expectations In Marriage

The expectations we develop over the years about marriage and our spouse have a great effect on our relationship. To have a good adjustment in marriage you must begin with realistic expectations of what marriage is and what each spouse should be.

Expectations are silent blueprints in our minds. Hope is defined as: "Expectation with desire." Therefore, these are silent "hopes" we have for our marriage. With realistic expectations we can succeed in making our marriage a success. Unrealistic expectation will cause us to fail.

Consider these UNREALISTIC expectations:

1. "Marriage will make me happy." Happiness only comes through mutual work and understanding of each partner.

2. "A good marriage has no problems." All marriages have disagreements and problems. Successful marriages communicate about these problems and work them out. But the KEY is commitment to your relationship.

3. "Material things make me happy." The Bible teaches just the opposite, and I agree! If you are happy only because of some material possession, you are on dangerous ground. There is tremendous value in learning how to suffer together as a couple, and working together to make financial ends meet. I have heard couples say over and over "how happy we were when we didn't have anything."

4. "The person we are about to marry is perfect." No one is perfect! Any person can disappoint you at one time or another. My spouse is not perfect, but she is MINE!

11

5. "Children will make us happy." Children are an added burden to a couple. They increase your expense, decrease your private time, are a drain on your energy, in general they are an interruption. But the couple who wants children for the right reasons and plan for them, will find children to be one of the greatest blessings of life.

6. "Christian marriages will last." Just because you marry a Christian doesn't mean that you automatically will succeed. Some have the tendency to let their guard down and not try as hard in their Christian marriage. A successful marriage comes from working at being the best partner you can be and staying committed to each other.

7. "I will be able to have my way all the time." Self-giving is the key to success in marriage. If you need to have "your way" all the time, your marriage is headed for all kinds of resentments.

Consider these REALISTIC expectations:

1. "The other person must be himself." The other person will not be what you want him to be if he is not already that way. You can't change a person by force or demands. Change can only come by love and acceptance of who they are.

2. "You have the ability to deal with the problems that arise." God made us in His image and we are capable. Whether it be serious illness of our spouse or children, loss of a job, adultery, etc., you can handle it with prayer.

3. "The time will come when I will have to shoulder up to my responsibility in the marriage." We all have to be responsible if we are to succeed.

4. "Life will change and as we live we will change also." Everyone changes in belief or understanding in all areas of life. Don't be surprised, but grow together. Change is a natural part of life and comes with time.

5. "True love, not capable as a teenager, does include physical attraction, emotional levels, and mutual interest." We will grow in our love.

6. "Both partners are *homemakers*." In our age both partners work outside the home, and therefore should share in the homemaking. It is not a put down to the male's manhood, but an expression of love as the leader of the home. Also, it is the man's responsibility.

The Christian Wife

Here are 10 commandments given to the wife:

1. Honor thine own womanhood, that thy days may be long and happy in thy house.
2. Expect not thy husband to give thee (at first) as many luxuries as thy father hath given thee after long years of hard labor and

sacrifice.

3. Forget not the virtue of good humor, for verily all that a man hath will he give for a woman's smile.
4. Thou shalt not nag.
5. Thou shalt seek well to please thy husband.
6. Remember that the frank approval of thy husband is worth more to thee than the sidelong glances of many strangers.
7. Forget not the grace of cleanliness and good dress.
8. Permit no one to assure thee that thou art having a hard time of it.
9. Keep thy home with all diligence, for out of it shall come the joys of thine old age.
10. Commit thy ways unto the Lord thy God, and thy children shall rise up and call thee blessed.

Author Unknown

The above writer has some very pratical advice for the wife. In this chapter, I will illustrate and explain some of these commands from my life experiences and from scripture.

Dr. Carl Brecheen and his wife conducted a survey among 50 couples they believed to have a good husband/wife relationship. These couples were all faithful Christians, and were asked to list, "The Qualities MOST Important In A Christian Wife." The following is the list they gave:

1. Personal relationship with God.
2. Affectionate (warm, responsive).
3. A good self-image.
4. Submissive to husband.
5. Patient
6. Loyal (dependable).
7. Right priorities.
8. Available to husband's physical needs.
9. Zest for living (joyful).
10. Unselfish.
11. Homemaker.
12. Good attitude (loving, cheerful, forgiving).
13. Not too materialistic.
14. Sense of Humor.
15. Outside interest.[1]

This is a very interesting list. It emphasizes what I believe to be some of the most important characteristics of a Christian wife. Number one is her spiritual relation to God. Numbers two and three, her feelings about herself will determine if she can be responsive to another person. Submission is so very important. The remainder of the list are qualities needed to have a successful husband/wife relationship.

Purpose Of Her Creation

In Genesis 2:18 is the story of why God created the woman. "It is not good that man should be alone; I will make him a HELPER COMPARABLE to him."

God had made everything in the world and he had described it as "Good." But when He came to man He looked at him and said it was "not good." Why? Because the man was alone. ALONE is a very tragic word.

So God made all the animals He had created pass in front of man to see if one was suitable for him. Surprise! None was found. I'm glad, aren't you! So God caused a deep sleep to come over man and He took a rib out of the side of man and made a helper for the man.

The word "helper" means:

COUNTERPART	- NOT -	OPPOSER (One of two parts that makes the whole.)
COMPLETOR	- NOT -	COMPETITOR
ADAPTER	- NOT -	SELF-SERVER
PROTECTOR	- NOT -	EXPOSER
PURSUER	- NOT -	TORMENTOR

The woman is to be the helper in all these areas. But in some cases she becomes just the opposite of what God intended.

Instead of the counterpart, she becomes the opposer. "Nor was man created for the woman; but woman for the man." 1 Corinthians 11:9.

Instead of the completor, she becomes the competitor. "An excellent wife is the crown of her husband." Proverbs 12:4a.

Instead of the adapter, she becomes the self-server. "Let nothing be done through selfish ambition or conceit, but in lowliness of mind let each esteem the other better than himself." Philippians 2:3.

Instead of the protector, she becomes the exposer. "There is one who speaks like the piercing of a sword, But the tongue of the wise promotes health." Proverbs 12:18.

Instead of the pursuer, she becomes the tormentor. "It is better to dwell in a corner of a housetop, Than in a house shared with a contentious woman." Proverbs 21:9.

The wife is a helper comparable with the man. So marriage is an adventure in togetherness. She is the final and finest portion of God's creation. All other creatures were created from nothing, but woman was created from a finished product, therefore by right of creation, woman at her best should surpass all the other creatures in the universe in grace, charm, tenderness, and poise. Unfortunately not all women are at their best.

Consider this advice given by a general's wife:

"If I were newly married I would do just what I did before. I would go ahead and have my family on my husband's small income, build friendships, see him start every morning with a hot breakfast, and do my best to help him achieve his ambitions whatever they might be."

This statement was made by Mrs. Dwight D. Eisenhower.

The passage ends in verse 24, "Therefore a man shall LEAVE his father and mother and be JOINED to his wife, and they shall become ONE FLESH." The two become one - a unit, a team. Therefore, the most important task before them is to make a home. Both are involved!

There are three important words in this verse:

1. LEAVE - This word indicates maturity, independence on the part of the young person. He or she is ready to make their own way. The divorce rate among teenage marriages is 85%. Only one out of ten teenage marriages works. When they do leave, parents don't cut the apron strings, untie them. You don't want to break all ties with your child. Let them go!

One college girl I knew wanted to get married. Her parents were against it, her sisters were against it. As a result of the strain, she married the man anyway, but the family was never the same. Parents let those children go!

2. JOINED - This word means, "welded together, glued together, something permanently joined together." Marriage is a commitment. In the Mississippi Delta we have an abundance of little green tree frogs. They stick to everything, even people. When I think of this word, I think of those green tree frogs.

A mother came to me and related the story of how she had almost destroyed her relationship with her children. She and her daughter had become so close that she was her daughter's best friend, and her daughter was hers. She dreamed of the day that her daughter would get married and had planned everything out. Well, her daughter eloped with a young man that the mother did not like.

The mother was devastated. She went into a depressed state that lasted for years. She did not want to see anyone. When she went to visit her daughter and son-in-law, the son-in-law would leave the house instead of facing her. Her husband tried to tell her she was driving her daughter away, but she would not listen.

Finally, she became so depressed that she tried to commit suicide. A neighbor found her almost dead. It was only at this point when she realized what she was doing to herself and her family. She began to take steps to build a better relationship with her son-in-law, and restore the strained relationship with her daughter and husband. Parents, let those children go!

3. ONE FLESH - This means more than the sexual union. Sex is a very important part of the union, or binding of the relationship. But,

15

"one flesh" goes further to include becoming a part of each other. I believe the idea is seen in verses like 1 Corinthians 7:1-7. Paul says the wife's body belongs to the husband and coversely. Also, Ephesians 5:28 says, Husbands ought to love their own wives as their own bodies.'" Each partner is so much a part of the other that each feels the other's body belongs to them. Now that is closeness!

In marriage the basic agreement is: One makes a living, freeing the other to function at home to make it the emotional hub of the family. The home is the most important thing for both husband and wife. Therefore, it is the center of activity and fulfillment. The wife is that hub even if she works outside the home. This is an important work, because no matter how rough or bad the world is, the children and the husband will come home to a loving, godly mother and wife. The world can't undo all the work and training of a godly mother.

If the husband comes home to a nagging wife, why come home? A great deal depends on the wife to make the home a place of love and acceptance.

One man I counseled with told how his wife would have the children lined up at the door for their spankings, and a list of jobs he had to do before bed time to greet him each day when he came home from work. Is it any wonder he went home later and later each day? Finally, he didn't go home at all. Everyone said, "What an awful man he is." But who is to blame?

Someone has suggested *the twelve most important minutes of the day*.[2] First four minutes, *when you wake up in the morning*. How you greet one another sets the tone for the day. If the wife gets up fussing about something, it will make both have a rotten day. Why not start out with a singing cheerful personality. You can if you choose to!

Second four minutes, *when the husband comes home from work*. Don't put all the problems of the day on him when he walks in the door. Let him know how happy you are to see him first. If you are happy to see him, he will be happy to see you. Later you can tell him about the problems.

Third four minutes, *the last thing you say before he leaves for work*. Don't be negative and tell him to try and accomplish something today. Express your confidence in him and his ability to achieve, and he will. He will think you are the greatest woman in the world, and you are!

Scriptural Instructions

The following verses of scripture are important Bible teachings for the wife:

1. **Husbands and wives are dependent on each other.** "Neither is man independent of woman, nor woman independent of man, in the

Lord. For as the woman was from the man, even so the man also is through the woman; but all things are from God." 1 Corinthians 11:11,12.

"Submitting to one another in the fear of God." Ephesians 5:21.

Both verses express the dependence husbands and wives have on each other. It is a mutual thing. Wives submit, while the husband is to love her as Christ loved the church. How did Christ love the church? What is His example?

In Matthew 20:25-28 Jesus said the greatest in the kingdom is the servant of all. Later he said He came not to be ministered to, but to minister to others. That is how Jesus loved the church, He served it! Husbands love in the same way!

Judy and I, after twenty years of marriage, have reached the point where we can't stand to be upset with each other. If we disagree about something, I can't wait to tell her it is all my fault, and she can't wait to say it is her fault. We smile and say, "It's not worth the hurt, I love you and please forgive me." We depend on each other!

2. **The principle of permanence.** "The woman who has a husband is bound by the law to her husband as long as he lives." Romans 7:2.

Some will say, "I don't love him anymore, I want a divorce." Love is not a feeling exclusively. Love is a decision! When you stop loving you made the decision to stop, because of certain circumstances. But lasting love is unconditional. It loves even when the other person hurts you. This love has made a commitment to the marriage. Love means the affirmation of the one loved and not the possession. The essential gift of love is a sense of self-worth. Therefore, love does not sustain marriage, but marriage sustains your love.

3. **Older women counsel younger women.** "The older women likewise, that they be reverent in behavior, not slanderers, not given to much wine, teachers of good things—that they admonish the younger women to love their husbands, to love their children, to be discreet, chaste, homemakers, good, obedient to their own husbands, that the word of God may not be blasphemed." Titus 2:3-5.

The older women are to be counselors and trainers of the younger women. This training is probably the teaching and example of a mother to her daughter, but it does not exclude older women in general teaching the younger women. It does assume that these older women have learned the lessons they are to teach the younger women.

These older women are to have the qualities of character and conduct described here. He mentions two temptations facing them. Probably because they are alone. Drinking too much wine, or drug use today, and becoming critics of the church and others. Paul contrasts the older women just described, to one of reverence, who seeks out avenues of service where she can do good works.

The root word for *lover* of her husband and children is phileo (to be a friend). The older women teach the younger women to be a friend, or lover of their husbands and children. This is not the unconditional love the husband is to have. She is his friend and helper. This word is a very interesting way to describe her love, and I believe it shows she is an emotional being.

4. **Things that win Husbands.** "Likewise you wives, be submissive to your own husbands, that even if some do not obey the word, they, without a word, may be won by the conduct of their wives, when they observe your chaste conduct accompanied by fear. Do not let your beauty be that outward adorning of arranging the hair, of wearing gold, or of putting on fine apparel; but let it be the hidden person of the heart, with the incorruptible ornament of a gentle and quiet spirit, which is very precious in the sight of God. For in this manner, in former times the holy women who trusted in God also adorned themselves, being submissive to their own husbands, as Sarah. . ." 1 Peter 3:1-6a.

The New Testament emphasizes the fact that the husband is the leader of the wife. Ephesians 5:22-24, Titus 2:5. So the wife here submits to her husband so she might win him for Christ by her behavior. This of course, recognizes the fact that the man is not a Christian.

The word "win" means to gain him for Christ. "Conduct" means her daily life, her attitudes, her actions toward him, every aspect of her life. The husband will see the effects of the gospel on the life of his wife and be moved to believe in Jesus.

Also, Peter considers where real beauty is found, the hidden person. Peter is not saying give no attention to your appearance or dress, but the inner person is the one to adorn with the imperishable jewels of a gentle and quiet spirit. "Gentle" means meek and mildness in temperament and patient endurance. "Quiet" suggests tranquility. Both attributes are very important for the wife in her relationship to her husband. I will discuss submission in a later chapter.

5. **Honor the wife.** "Likewise you husbands, dwell with them with understanding, giving honor to the wife, as to the weaker vessel, and as being heirs together of the grace of life, that your prayers may not be hindered." 1 Peter 3:7.

Husbands are to honor their wives. There are many ways he can do this. I will discuss more about this in the next chapter. Here are a few:

1. Stand when she enters the room, a sign of respect.
2. Take off your hat in her presence.
3. Offer her your seat when none are left.

4. Speak respectfully to her all the time.

5. Show her your love by actions and attitudes.

I believe wives can do things to earn this type of respect and honor from their husbands. Some women do very peculiar things. For example, some study English grammar to learn to speak correctly and then turn around and blemish their lips with profanity and filthy, vulgar speech that makes you heartsick to hear it.

In America women spend, conservatively, five billion dollars a year on cosmetics to make themselves beautiful. Then they turn around and smoke which contaminates their breath, discolors their skin, and stains their teeth. I don't believe anyone who smokes is the example for Christ they could be. With all the statistics about cancer and smoking there is a strong case for it being a sin. 1 Corinthians 3:16, 17.

6. **Dress modestly.** "Women adorn themselves in modest apparel, with propriety. . .which is proper for women professing godliness, with good works." 1 Timothy 2:9,10.

What is modest dress? It is any clothing that does not unduly reveal the figure of the wearer, or that would cause a man to lust after her. It may be clothing that is too low in the neckline, too short, too thin, too tight, or too revealing. Wives, I encourage you to dress as Christian women of God.

7. **Supreme homemaker.** A joyful singing home personality includes practical things like meals. Nothing reflects the personality of the wife like the appearance of the home. It doesn't have to be luxurious, but just neat and clean. I believe this is an essential role for the wife. Of course, the husband can help. If the wife works he should take some of the load, but the wife is still the chief homemaker.

Edith Johnson in **Why Don't Women Keep Their Men?** said:

"Far too many men are coming home from a tense business world and entering into homes filled with that same tense atmosphere. The wife who complains that the world is treating her shabbily, that her wardrobe is too skimpy, that her cares are too many, and her pleasures are too few, is but adding to the emotional strain under which the husband may rebel at any time. Or, she may demand that he take her out socially when he is too tired to keep going. If our people would discard the foolish notion that a man's worth is measured by the amount of money he makes, or the social position that he attains, then fewer men would go to an early grave."

Wives you are the key to success in the marriage. I pray all these suggestions will help you achieve the goals you want for you and your spouse.

19

Questions

1. What are some unrealistic expectations for marriage that you would like to emphasize?

2. What qualities in a wife do you feel are most important and would add to the list?

3. What qualities do you have that help you to succeed as a wife?

4. What scriptures speak most to the needs you have as a Christian wife? Why do you feel they apply to you?

5. What would you do differently if you could start your marriage over?

[1]Carl Brecheen and Paul Faulkner, **What Every Family Needs,** Austin, Texas: Sweet Publishing Company, 1979.

[2]Clifton Rogers, "The Happy Christian Home," A paper presented at the Harding College Lectureship.

CHAPTER 3

The Christian Husband

This chapter will consider the man in the role of husband exclusively. In a later chapter I will consider the man in the role of father.

Dr. Robert Blood and Dr. Donald Wolfe of the University of Michigan interviewed more than 900 American wives about their satisfaction with their husband's relationship. They found:

1. Women want companionship from their husbands even more than they want love and/or money.
2. Children, far from bringing a marriage closer together, are one of the major causes for loss of satisfaction in each other's companionship and love.
3. Nearly all the wives were becoming increasingly less satisfied with their husband's companionship, a decline that researchers described as corrosive.

Also, in a Gallup Poll, when asked, "If you could have a different spouse than the one you have now, would you?" Nine of ten men said, "NO!" Nine of ten women said, "YES!"

Husbands, something is definitely wrong! I believe that men and their attitudes about marriage are the major source of the problem. God has given the husband four major responsibilities to the marriage!

To Lead

"But I want you to know that the head of every man is

21

Christ, the head of woman is man, and the head of Christ is God." 1 Corinthians 11:3.

This is God's line of authority in the marriage. It doesn't teach that women are inferior to men, but it does teach a line of responsibility. In a later chapter I will discuss the teaching of Bible submission.

Alexander Schneiders in his book, **Roles and Role Relationship In Marriage** said of the husband's leadership:

"The husband should be a dominant figure in the life of his family, even though he should not be dominating. He should be a leader without being a dictator. He should be the. . .head of the home, while carefully preserving the equal rights and privileges of his wife. He should be the decision-maker, after careful and thorough consultation and agreement with his partner. Without these basic characteristics, it is extremely doubtful whether any man can fulfill the role of husband."

The husband is to assume his leadership role, not just demand it. He is to develop the capacity to lead. His authority is not his, it is given to him by God. It is a gift, and he is to be a good steward of this gift.

Consider these principles of ASSUMED leadership. The scriptural basis is Luke 22:24-30. The disciples were arguing about who was considered the greatest among them. Jesus said, "The kings of the Gentiles exercise lordship over them, and those who exercise authority over them are called 'benefactors.' But not so among you; on the contrary, he who is greatest among you, let him be as the younger, and he who GOVERNS as he who SERVES. . .I am among you as the One who serves. . ." The one who GOVERNS is like the one who SERVES! What Jesus is talking about is the servant/leader ruler. When I lead my family or wife, as God intended, I become the greatest servant in the family. I am not the lord that bosses everyone around. I am the servant. What a beautiful picture of a man's relationship to his wife and children.

For the husband to receive submission from his wife and children, he has to demonstrate submission himself. He demonstrates submission to God by his obedience to God's commands. Philippians 2:5-8. He demonstrates submission to the government by obeying the laws of the land. Romans 13:1-7. He demonstrates submission to his employer by hard work, and being respectful of his employer. Ephesians 6:5. If he doesn't show submission in his life, he will not get it from his wife and children.

What causes a wife to react?[2]

1. When he fails to be the spiritual leader - she is insecure.

2. When he allows problems to continue and even get worse - she takes matters into her own hands.
3. When he doesn't support her discipline of the children - she loses respect for him.
4. When he doesn't accept himself - she doesn't either.
5. When he admires other women - she feels inferior and jealous.
6. When he verbalizes love only when he wants a physical relation - she feels she is being used.
7. When he doesn't spend time talking with her - she feels alone and finds others to talk to.
8. When he forgets anniversaries and other special occasions - she feels she is not important to him.
9. When he fails to notice the little extra things she does for him - she loses her creativity for her husband and home.
10. When he is not alert to dangers she faces - she is lead astray.

For us to be a leader of our wife and family, we have to be MEN! Men as God wants us to be.

1. We will be men that are *true to God's standards*. We claim to be Bible believers, but do we really stand for God? If the government required you to do something that was a clear violation of scripture, what would you do?

On two occasions Daniel was faced with that dilemma. Daniel 1:8-15; Daniel 6:7-12. On one occasion Daniel explained his convictions to the officer in charge and respectfully asked to follow a creative alternative. Permission was given and it proved to be a good solution.

On the second occasion he had to choose either to submit to God's teachings or submit to the physical consequences of disobedience to the king's command. His spiritual convictions caused him to obey God and God used this incident to bring honor and great things to His people.

A man that doesn't know God's principles has no basis for discerning spiritual dangers. When he doesn't live by the principles of God, he sows the seeds of destruction for his own personal life, his family, and his wife. These principles are not optional. No person, no church, no nation can continue to violate them and not experience conflict as a result.

So the wise man is one who knows the principles, and chooses to follow them, whatever the cost - that is conviction!

2. We will be men who are *aware of the spiritual dangers facing our wives and children.*

Consider Samson. He was given supernatural power by God. Yet he was conquered by a woman, blinded by his enemies, and forced to grind grain in a prison. Because he rejected the authority of his parents, and God's warnings, and did his own will.

Samson saw a girl that he wanted. He told his parents to get her for him. Manoah tried to reason with his son, but he rebelled, "Get her for me, for she pleases me well." Judges 14:3.

Manoah should have been aware of the spiritual dangers his son faced in life. He could have helped Samson take on better standards. God calls for husbands and fathers to be alert! 1 Peter 5:8.

How? Men need to be aware of associations, temptations, worldly motives and conflicts that face each member of the family. Do you know the falsehoods your wife is being exposed to everyday? What books does she read, T.V. programs does she watch, all plant seed thoughts in her mind. I don't mean be a dictator and tell your wife everything she can read or watch on T.V., but as the spiritual leader you should be aware of what is influencing her and teaching her, so you can help her see the ways of God.

The husband is to be his wife's major teacher. You need to know what teaching in scripture she needs to help her grow spiritually. If you can't teach her, then why should she listen to you? You have to be a man that knows the Word.

The same is true of your children. What philosophies are they being taught in school? What do their teachers believe? Who are their friends, and what kind of an influence are they?

Be a man for God, and stand for Him!

3. We will be men when we *apply scriptural convictions to our own lives, whatever the cost.* A man is a man when he stands for God, and makes the needed changes in his own life to meet his convictions.

Joshua was promised by God that he would be prosperous and successful in everything he did, if he would be faithful to ONE ACTIVITY.

God makes that same promise to us, if we will do this ONE ACTIVITY. We will be wiser than our enemies, have more understanding than all our teachers. What is the activity? To MEDITATE on God's WORD and APPLY IT to our daily lives.

"This Book of the Law shall not depart from your mouth, but you shall meditate in it day and night, that you may observe to do according to all that is written in it. For then you will make your way prosperous and then you will have good success." Joshua 1:8.

How can we demonstrate we are men of conviction?

(1. **Be strong in our purpose.** We should make it exciting for our families to build their faith on the Word of God. We should be committed to the spiritual success of every family member.

(2. **Be strong in grace.** By grace I mean the attribute of God. But, He gives us His grace by the love of His son. Jo. 3:16. His grace in us is

the desire we have and the power we have to do His will. "By the grace of God I am what I am, and His grace toward me was not in vain. But I labored more abundantly than they all, yet not I, but the grace of God which was with me." 1 Corinthians 15:10.

Grace in Paul enabled him to do the things he did for Christ, to labor for the Lord.

How do we get it? By humbling ourself before God. "God resists the proud, But gives grace to the humble!" James 4:6.

His grace gives us the desire and the power to keep God's Word in our daily lives.

(3. **Be strong in God's Spirit.** "He would grant you. . .to be strengthened with might through His Spirit in the inner man." Ephesians 3:16b.

What does that mean? That we develop in our lives the fruits of the Spirit. Galatians 5:22,23. These fruits help us to grow and understand the deeper teachings and ways of God.

We can discern the wrong attitudes and ideas in our lives and the lives of others. And we will know how to respond to them in love. We will motivate them to make daily application of these principles in their lives. Hebrews 10:24.

(4. **We will be men when we are strong in faith.** Faith is defined as, "The substance of things hoped for, the evidence of things not seen." Hebrews 11:1. Being sure and certain of what we hope for is faith.

Faith is the capacity of the human heart, when activated by the word of god, that enables a man or a woman who has not seen God to know without a doubt that He is real.

I am not saying that faith makes the unreal real. That is a fairy tale -"Star Wars." Christianity is REAL! Faith makes the unseen real!

Faith is being SURE of what we hope for. The greek word is *hupostasis* which means, "That which stands under something else or provides the basis for something." The same word is used in Hebrews 1:3 to say of Jesus that he is the "express image" of God. Applied to faith, it is seeing a visible reality of what we are hoping for. We know it is real.

Faith deals with things we can't see, but by faith you know they are real. If you must see the end of a matter before you begin it, there is no faith in that. Our senses relate to the visible, but faith relates to the invisible. It takes man beyond the boundaries of the physical world to the invisible, to God. At conversion we are changed from seeing the visible, only, to seeing the invisible. We no longer trust wholly in ourselves, but in God. "We walk by faith, not by sight." 2 Corinthians 5:7.

Following are seven skills an effective spiritual leader must have.

1. You must be in a continual state of GRATEFULNESS to the Lord. A husband's gratefulness is what promotes an atmosphere of gratefulness in the family. As the family sees him express his gratefulness, they will follow suit. A basic aspect of greatfulness is the spirit of CONTENTMENT.

2. You must have a genuine spirit of HUMILITY. God is working with a fallible and weak person. Our past failures are a key means of reminding us that there is no room for pride on our part. Every husband should maintain in the back of his mind a sanctified "Hall of Shame." This humble spirit must carry over to those we love. The husband must show his need for his wife and each of the children. And they need to hear you say you love them and need them.

3. You must learn to CONTROL your TONGUE and EMOTIONS. The members of the family want to see a husband that is consistent, one they can count on. They become discouraged if they see dad up one day and down the next. I know that is hard to control, but they need and expect continual encouragement and reassurance from him.

4. You must have GOOD MANNERS. What I mean by manners is continual sacrifice for the family. The husband makes sure that everyone's needs are taken care of before his own. His manners demonstrate his love for the family to the world.

5. You must ACCEPT each person where he or she is. Each child will develop at his own rate. The father must give a balance of supervision and freedom to let each child grow. Too much freedom or too much supervision will be interpreted by the child as rejection. Find the balance that works for each of your children.

6. A father must recognize individual WORTH and POTENTIAL. He must see both the strong and weak points of each person in the family. Emphasize the strong points and see how you can provide the training to strengthen the weak points.

7. He must earn the RIGHT TO BE HEARD. You can't expect to be heard just because you are a father and husband. You earn that right! How? By spending time and energy on developing a good relationship with each family member. So work on it!

To Love

"Husbands, love your wives, just as Christ also loved the church. . ." Ephesians 5:25.

The husband is to love his wife more than his parents. He has a responsibility to his wife more than any other person. "Therefore a man shall leave his father and his mother and be joined to his wife and they shall become one flesh." Genesis 2:24. This doesn't mean the man forgets his parents. It simply means to love your wife *more*. I will have just as much chance to go to heaven, if I refused to repent of some sin, as if I refused to love my wife more than any other person on earth. The same is true for the wife and her parents, and our love for our own children. They may take more of our time in the beginning of their lives, but my love for my wife is to be the greatest love of all. How much am I to love my wife? "Husbands, love your wives just as Christ loved the church, and gave Himself for it." Ephesians 5:25. God put some emphasis on the love of a husband for his wife when He said, "as Christ loved the church." How did He love the church? He gave Himself for the church.

"Husbands ought to love their own wives as their own bodies. . .for no one ever hated his own flesh, but nourishes and cherishes it." Ephesians 5:28,29. What a statement to men about the love and care they are to provide their wives. Love includes showing our affection and concern for the other person.

Husbands exercise their bodies to build muscles, stand in front of the mirror and admire how handsome they look. Husbands spend time shaving, bathing, and combing their hair, all to show their love for themselves. I believe all of these same things show love for the wife. He admires her, cares for her, satisfied her needs whatever they are, expresses to her how beautiful she is, encourages her, is attentive to her, and so on.

Love is more than a feeling, it is something we learn. Dr. Menninger said:

". . .the child does not automatically know how to love. . .unless we teach our children how to love, and we in turn know how to love, we never become a contributing social being."[3]

Love is something we learn to express and feel. Someone had defined love as: (1. A decision - you decide to love. (2. A choice - you choose to love as opposed to hate. (3. A gift - you give yourself to another person.

What is love? Scripture defines it:

"This love of which I speak is slow to lose patience; it looks for a way of being constructive; it is not possessive; it is neither anxious to impress nor does it cherish any inflated ideas of its own importance. Love has good manners and does not pursue selfish advantage; it is not touchy; it does not compile statistics of evil, nor does it gloat over wickedness in other people, but on the contrary, true love rejoices with all good men when truth prevails. Love knows no limits to its hope. It can outlast

27

anything. It is in fact the one thing that still stands when all else has fallen." 1 Corinthians 13:4-8. (Phillips).

Consider each of the characteristics mentioned in this passage. It is an exhaustive list of what love is. Those who love will exhibit most of these characteristics depending on the degree of their love. I believe I have grown in many of these characteristics since the time I first met my wife of twenty-three years.

Judy and I were reading some of my old love letters from our college days. They were really mushy. But I watched a gleam come in Judy's eyes as she read those words and I realized again how much that time of courtship and those words of endearment meant to her and still do.

Husbands, express that love to your wife! One woman said, "When I ask my husband, 'Do you love me?' he thinks I am asking for information." Wives need action and words. The five most important words for a husband to say to his wife are: "I love you very much."

One question arises, "What do I do when love grows cold, can it be rekindled?" I believe it can, if there is any desire to do so on the part of both spouses. Again, love is something we learn. Love comes when we act like we love. It is easier to act like you love, than it is to feel like it. When you act out your love for another, and for yourself, over a period of time, you will grow to feel like loving that person again. It will be rekindled.

Rabbi Akiba said, "Make your wife the most beautiful woman in your life and she will be."

The key to love is commitment. The word used in 1 Corinthians 13 is the greek word *agape*. It means to love as God loves us. God loved us when we were sinners. He gave Himself for us when we did not deserve it. He loved us in spite of what we had done. When partners in marriage love unconditionally, there is nothing the other person can do that will destroy that love or commitment you have to each other.

To Live Considerately With

"Likewise you husbands, dwell with them with understanding, giving honor to the wife, as to the weaker vessel, and as being heirs together of the grace of life, that your prayers may not be hindered." 1 Peter 3:7.

What does the word UNDERSTANDING mean: considerate, investigative, insightful, sensitive. Very simply stated it means the husband will study his wife to see what her needs are. It is obvious that some men are real *clods* in this matter of consideration. Some men will spend thousands of dollars to research their business, but will spend neither time nor money to research the needs of their wives.

28

How would you answer the following questions:

1. What are some of my wife's most wanted needs?
2. What makes her happy?
3. What makes her nervous?
4. What makes her relaxed?
5. What makes her depressed?

How you answer these questions shows your knowledge of your wife's needs.

James Dodson gives the list of things that cause depression in women.[4]

1. Low self-esteem
2. Fatigue and time pressure
3. Loneliness and isolation
4. Absence of romantic love
5. Financial difficulties
6. Sex problems
7. Menstrual and physiological problems
8. Problems with children
9. Aging

Husbands need to be aware of these things that cause depression and help their wives overcome them as they arise in their lives.

Husbands particularly need to be considerate when the children are ill, or the wife is ill, some husbands I know have asked their sick wives to get up out of bed and wait on them. How inconsiderate can a person be! Also, husbands need to be considerate when it is "that time of the month" for her. Someone said, "For some strange reason human beings, and particularly women, can tolerate stress and pressure much more easily if at least one other person knows they are enduring it."

Sweet Sue wrote "Dear Abby":

> "My heart doesn't yearn for wall-to-wall carpeting and fancy clothes, but Oh, Abby, how I would love to have my husband bring home some foolish little gift on some unspecial day. He's not a thoughtless guy, but when you have to 'hint' it's no fun. He's a grand guy and a wonderful husband, and if he'd only do this little thing to let me know I am as special to him as he is to me, I'd be the happiest woman in the world."

Sweet Sue is not alone in her desire to feel special to the man she loves.[5]

Also, little things are important to your wife:

- Dates such as birthdays and anniversaries
- Patience

- Truthfulness
- Praise, she needs lots of it for the things she does for you and the family. The homemakers only source of praise is the husband.
- Gentleness and tenderness
- Don't over criticize
- Ask her regularly what you can do to help, or better yet, do it without being asked.
- Breakfast in bed
- Courtesy, "love in trifles"

Husbands need to show courtesy to their wives. Most men are courteous in public, to business associates, and friends. Why not then to the most important person in your life? I know the hardest thing for a husband to say to his wife is - "I am sorry." I believe it is a matter of pride, but it should not be. A husband should be able to humble himself before his wife if he expects her to submit to him.

Husbands need to learn some two word phrases: "Thank you," "Excuse me," "Pardon me," etc.

Another teaching in this verse is that the husband should honor his wife. Peter gives three reasons we should honor her.

1. Peter tells us too, "Give honor to the wife." God created woman in His own image, therefore she deserves my highest admiration and respect. Genesis 1:27.

Man should not abuse the gift that God has given him. Genesis 3:12. Abraham tried to get Sarah to lie for him and as a result God was displeased. Genesis 12:11-20. We should make up our minds that our wives are to have a special place of permanent honor in our hearts and lives.

2. Peter said because she is the weaker of the two. This does not mean inferior, but generally physically weaker. I realize some women are physically stronger than some men, but generally that is not true. The wife is to be protected by her husband.

3. Peter said, "that your prayers may not be hindered." It is important for the Christian husband to realize how he treats his wife has a direct effect on his relationship to God. If he mistreats her, his prayers will not be answered and his good relationship to God will be put in jeopardy.

To Support The Family

"If anyone does not provide. . .especially for those of his household, he has denied the faith and is worse than an unbeliever." 1 Timothy 5:8.

As a husband, I am to support my family. I believe that when you marry you pledge all you have and all you ever hope to have to the support of your home. Whether the wife works outside the home or not the man has a duty to see that his family is cared for.

What hurts me the most is to see a father that is shrinking this duty. I have gone into homes as a minister and found children literally starving for food and without clothing while their father would be in the next room passed out from drinking away his income. I have seen parents spend $30 to $40 a week on cigarettes and deny their children sufficient food to eat. I have seen men that would lie around their apartment all day claiming to be sick, but were just too lazy to find a job.

The husband that does such as this has no right to have a wife and children. God has decreed that he is worse than an UNBELIEVER.

I realize that some men have been forced into the position that they can't financially take care of their families. Maybe because of serious illness, or an accident, or loss of a job, they are unable to work as they desire. I believe God understands that, but it is the slothful man that God is condemning.

By the grace of God I am able to work and take care of my family. If I ever get in the position that I can't provide for my family and someone has to do without, it will be me before anyone else. I am thankful that I can work and provide.

Let me close this chapter with these observations:
1. The husband is the leader, not the dictator of the home.
2. The husband is the one God made responsible for the family - but he is not superior.
3. The husband makes the final decision, but he is not the exclusive decision maker.
4. The husband is the leader, but he is not always right.
5. The husband is a lover.
6. The husband can ask for submission ONLY after he has submitted himself.
7. The husband will be considerate of his wife and family.

Questions

1. Do you agree with the statement: "The husband should be a dominant figure, even though he should not be dominating." Discuss "servant/leader" leadership in the family. As a husband how do you lead your family?

2. How can a husband teach his wife? Is this important?

3. How do you express your love for your wife? Make a list of suggestions that will be helpful to new husbands.

4. What ways do you express your consideration for your wife? Has

your wife ever accused you of being inconsiderate? Did you believe her?

[1]Mid McKnight, **Vestibules of Heaven,** Abilene, Texas: McKnight Publications.

[2]**Men's Manual,** Oak Brook, Illinois: Institute In Basic Youth Conflicts, Inc.

[3]Karl Menninger, **Love Against Hate,** New York: Harcourt, Brace, and World, 1942. (A Harvest Book)

[4]James Dodson, **What Wives Wish Their Husbands Know About Women,** Wheaton, Illinois: Tyndale Press, 1975.

[5]Clifton Rogers, "The Happy Christian Home," A Paper presented at the Harding College Lectureship.

CHAPTER 4

Love In The Home

W hat do you mean when you say to your spouse, "I love you?" Are you saying, "I want to have sex;" or "I enjoy being with you;" or "You are a special person to me;" or "You are the most important person in my life." Love between a husband and wife has to be more than just a physical attraction for the marriage to last.

Karl Menninger in his book, *Love Against Hate* quotes Ferenczi about love:

"They want to love one another, but they don't know how. Frustrated and hungry for a word, a touch, a smile, a shared experience that would satisfy this universal hunger, many people try feverishly to fill the void with semblances of love - activity, popularity, philanthropy, prestige - there are thousands of ways of extracting recognition in lieu of love, none of them satisfactory."

This statement was written about the masses of people that are looking for a feeling of belonging or love. If the church could become more knowledgeable about love and how to communicate it to individuals so that they could understand it, those that are seeking love would come running to Christ who truly lived it and of whom we preach.

But the sad truth is that too often this love is not applied to the Christian home. When the need for love goes unfulfilled, or is only partially fulfilled, loneliness is the first result. If it continues to be unfulfilled it leads to depression, or hostility, or physical illness, or mental illness, or even death. All of these stages can be seen in homes where unfulfilled love is found.

Consider this counseling session with a young girl. She is describing her home and the lack of affection she feels. Does it sound like your home?

"I have no place in my family. When I go home, I am treated like - not - not good, not bad. I wish that my father or mother would fuss or even scream at me. Then I would know that they knew I was there. I can't stand being treated like I wasn't there at all. Mom's like that because dad's like that, and she is scared of him. I go home when I have to, mostly on holidays. When I go home, I walk in and say, 'Hello,' and when I leave I say, 'Goodbye.' It is like I am a guest in a motel, checking in and checking out."

In this session she talked about a friend's home and the difference she felt when she visited with them.

"From the time I walked in, I could tell there was warmth, love, and concern. Her mother came around and asked everyone what they would like for supper. My friend's father was a policeman. The whole family was concerned about him. When he came home from work, they would all meet him at the door and make on over him."

It is obvious that this young girl was starving for love and feeling that she belonged. She saw so much love and affection in her friend's home and none in her home. She commented that her friend's parents would sit down together and talk out their problems.

This problem, as so many are in the family, is a matter of unfulfilled love, of belongingness, or self-respect. This girl needed to feel loved by her family.

Love Defined

I am not referring to LOVE as the average person uses it. In the world today we use the word love so much that is has become meaningless.

There are eight categories of NEEDS that most people have. They are: physical needs, safety needs, love needs, self-respect needs, information needs, understanding needs, beauty needs, and self-actualization needs. If anyone of these needs is satisfied, we normally say, "I just love _____" whatever it is.

For example, in the physical category, if we eat some food we like, we say, "I just love those fries!" The love and belongingness I am referring to is not this type of love.

It is not just sexual love. Although it can be included. The Bible refers to the sexual need as being fulfilled in a scriptural marriage. The sexual desires and drives in both men and women are pure and

34

holy in marriage and are not considered shameful. Paul in 1 Corinthians 7:1-7 and Ephesians 5:22-23 gives some important teaching about love and sex in the marriage. The husband belongs to the wife and his duty is to fulfill her sexual desires. The same is true of the wife. By the sexual relationship the "one flesh" relationship is created. It is essential to commitment in a marriage.

But, that kind of love and belongings I am referring to is something everyone can experience. There are basically two greek words that convey the total meaning of this love and belongingness: **Agape** and **Phileo.**

Agape is, "love that can be known only from the actions it prompts." God's love is seen in the gift of His son. It is not an impulse prompted by feelings. It does not always run with the natural inclinations, nor does it spend itself only upon those for whom some affinity is discovered. Love seeks the welfare of all.

Phileo represents tender affection. It is never used in a command for man to love God. It is an emotion. When one practices agape, phileo is developed.

When the Bible commands the husband to love his wife (Ephesians 5) the greek word for love is *agape.* When the wife is taught to love her husband (Titus 2:4) the greek word for love is *phileo.* The wife's love is an emotional love. But when the scripture teaches us to love our neighbor (Matthew 22:39) the greek word for love is *agape.* Agape is love known by the actions it prompts. It is unconditional love, "I love you in spite of what you do."

How To Express Love

The big question is, "how do we express that love to each other in our families?" I want to be as practical as I can.

1. Karl Menninger makes this statement:

"In the vast majority of instances our love for one another is expressed in non-physical ways, in the interchange of ideas, or the common enjoyment of some pleasure. One of the time honored forms is the ritual of eating together, or drinking together. Being given food is the first expression of love which the child understands."

Consider what he is saying about FOOD and LOVE. I had a friend in Fort Smith, Arkansas who expressed something very similar. He said, "You really get to know a person when you eat with them." He was talking about the closeness you feel, the acceptance you feel, you are a friend because you are sharing food together.

I believe this thought opens up a great new meaning for us as we eat the *Lord's Supper* in our worship services, or have *fellowship* meals at the church building. Jesus called himself the "Bread of Life." John 6. The New Testament church engaged in LOVE FEASTS before their Sunday worship assemblies. Jude 12, 2 Peter 2:13, 1 Corinthians 11:17-34. Yet in some churches they frown on the practice of Christians eating together in the church building. Eating together is an expression of our love for each other. When we are told to discipline a member and withdraw our fellowship the command is, "Not even to eat with such a person." 1 Corinthians 5:11b. Paul is describing an incident where a church is withholding its love from an unruly member. What better way to show it.

Also, when Jesus showed His love for sinners He ate with them. Matthew 9:11. He even fed 5000 hungry sinners. Mark 6:42.

What is this principle saying to the family about how to express our love? Many families have withdrawn from each other. They never eat together. The words are spoken, "I love you," but in reality the person is saying, "I love you, but I don't want to eat with you."

What is the mother saying to her family when she is always too tired to fix breakfast, or lunch, or even supper for the family? What is she saying when she tells them to please eat some place else?

What is the husband saying who is continually late for meals, or stops and eats before he comes home?

I realize this is a small point, but it does prove, "They want to love one another, but they don't know how."

2. Another practical way we express our love is by talking to each other. Included in this is listening. James says, "be swift to hear. . ." James 1:19.

Talking is the best therapy for a person with problems. He doesn't necessarily want any advice from you, but just to have someone listen to him and sympathize with him. A husband can break his wife with the silent treatment. He sticks his nose in the T.V., or the paper, or spends all his free time on some hobby and never talks to her. He is saying by his actions, "I hate you, don't bother me." People need other people to talk to on the deepest level of communication.

There are basically three levels of communication:

1. When you talk about things or ideas or events.
2. When you talk about non-significant groups.
3. When you talk about self and your emotions. How you feel, your hurts, joys, fears, shames, successes, and disappointments.

Some husbands and wives have never talked on level three. She doesn't know how he feels because he has never told her. He doesn't know her hopes and fears because he has never asked. How can they love each other if they don't really know each other? They can't!

Consider God's commands to the husband in Ephesians 5:25-30. In light of this passage, which of the statements below correctly describe how a husband should demonstrate his love for his wife.

___ By asserting his God ordained authority over her.

___ By always taking the initiative to restore a strained or broken relationship, no matter who is at fault.

___ By sacrifically spending himself for her.

— By loving her affectionately and physically.

— By making her spiritual welfare the first priority of their relationship.

___ By having her remain in her place in the home.

___ By encouraging her and assisting her to become all that God wants her to be.

All of these statements are part of the way a husband demonstrates his love. Because he is the leader and lover of his wife, the way he loves will influence the love of the whole family.

Paul in Titus 2:4,5, lists some ways a young woman can demonstrate her love.

"Admonish the younger women to love their husbands, to love their children, to be discreet, chaste, homemakers, good, obedient to their own husbands, that the word of God may not be blasphemed."

Solomon has given these qualities of a wife of noble character: loyal, good reputation, industrious, thrifty, good homemaker, good business person, healthy, charitable, strong, dignity, wisdom, called blessed by her children and husband. Proverbs 31:10-31.

Peter tells the wife to be concerned about INNERBEAUTY. 1 Peter 3:1-6. Why? Because the qualities she develops on the inside will determine the quality of love and care she will give to her husband and family and self.

I encourage you to ask each other the following question: "What is it that I do for you that makes you feel loved?" To answer, take a piece of paper and write down, "I feel loved when you _____ " at the top of the page, and then list as many answers as you can. Your list will be long and some of the answers will reveal to you many important things you do to make your spouse feel loved. Keep them up!

In 1 Corinthians 13:4-8, Paul lists the characteristics of unconditional love - agape. It is the love that lasts no matter what the spouse does.

"Love suffers long and is kind; love does not envy; love does not parade itself, is not puffed up; does not behave rudely, does not seek its own, is not provoked, thinks no evil; does not rejoice in

iniquity, but rejoices in the truth; bears all things, believes all things, hopes all things, endures all things. Love never fails."

I can't think of a better list than this to describe love. It can be applied to friendship, belongingness, affection, and unconditional love. I believe the sooner we start showing this type of love, the sooner we will help our children see what real love is. Love and belongingness can be easily seen in the families that have it and those that don't.

These are only two ways to communicate love in our homes. Some others are: giving of our time to another person, kind words, remembering special days, doing hobbies together, breakfast in bed, weekly dates, flowers at work, a special week of remembrance, special trips, family devotionals, etc. You get the point!

Let us not fail our families, but begin now to show them how much we love each one of them.

Questions

1. When you say "I love You," to your spouse, what do you mean by that statement? Be specific.

2. How do you express your love for your spouse? Give a list of ways you feel might be helpful to other spouses.

3. In the list of "Needs that most people have", on page 34, which one do you feel is the most important for you? Why?

4. Why is open, honest communication between a husband and wife so important for building their love for each other?

5. Do you feel that your love is growing for your spouse? Why and what are you doing to make it grow?

CHAPTER 5

The Need For Self-Esteem

A husband and wife are driving down the street in their car. They came to an intersection and she turns the corner short and the rear wheel jumps the curb.

"I told you that you are always hitting the curb," the husband said angrily.

"I don't either, just be quiet and leave me alone," she said in response.

Another husband comes home from work and finds the dishwasher broke down and his wife upset.

"Honey, come here and look at this dishwasher," she said.

"What's wrong?"

"I don't know. It just won't work. You are going to fix it aren't you?" she asks.

"I don't know, let me look at it. I don't think I can," he responds.

"Well, Sally's husband is always fixing things around their house. You mean to tell me you can't fix a little ole dishwasher?" she questioned.

Sound familiar? Scenes like these happen everyday. No wonder our self-esteem is hurting. Both spouses did all the wrong things to build their partners self-worth, and as a result bad feelings and resentment develop.

In chapter four, I mentioned eight basic needs that everyone has. They are: physical needs, (air, food, water, rest, sex, etc.), safety needs, love-belongingness, self-respect needs, information needs, understanding needs, beauty needs, and self-actualization needs.

These needs have to be fulfilled for a person to be happy and well-adjusted. The need I want to consider in this chapter is SELF-RESPECT.

Some have the mistaken idea that when one of these needs is fulfilled that it will never need to be fulfilled again.

For example, the need of HAPPINESS. Some spend all their lives looking for happiness, feeling that once they find it, it will always be theirs. This is not true! Each of these needs has to be fulfilled over and over again, just like the physical need of eating.

Another point is the principle of OVERSATURATION. When a need is fulfilled and it feels good, some want to fulfill it again, immediately. What happens? It is not as enjoyable the second time as it was the first time. If you continue to fulfill that need, it can lose all pleasure and even become something you hate. Oversaturation of anything can be harmful. Parents need to understand this in their relationship with their children, and each other.

A deprived need hurts, but an oversaturated need does not bring pleasure!

Now consider SELF-RESPECT. This need is second only to love-belongingness. Kauffman said, "A basic sense of one's own value, not vanity or false pride, but a proper sense of self regard. . .(is important) . . .that one is a SELF that is worth being."

Probably we would call it GUILT when a person has a lack of self-esteem. When we lack it we feel bored, tired, listless, depressed, "blue." We say, "What's the use anyway."

Children who need this need fulfilled will literally fight, tremble, use defense mechanisms as attention getters, negativism, isolation, fantasy, regression, or running away. Of course, we all agree that such responses are not good. But, these children need help to fulfill this need and develop a better self-esteem.

To an extent we all depend on others to help in this need. By their praise, honor, and concern we feel better about ourselves. Maturity is realizing the way you should act to get others to respect you. We need this type of praise and honor from others, both verbal and non-verbal.

A child who receives only correction and ridicule develops the attitude that he is no good and helpless. He becomes discouraged as a result. "You can do better than that," is not the most encouraging thing you can say to your child. Please don't fall into the trap of saying, "You did a good job, BUT. . ."

Self-respect is fulfilled by:
1. Living up to one's values.
2. Producing something needed by other humans.
3. Maintaining discipline, first by self, and second by others.

Stanley Coopersmith did a study on self-respect in children.[1] He said,

> "We found, not very surprisingly, that youngsters with a high degree of self-esteem are active, expressive individuals, who tend to be successful both academically and socially...In contrast, the boys with low self-esteem present a picture of discouragement and depression. They felt isolated, unlovable, incapable of expressing or defending themselves and too weak to confront or overcome their deficiencies. They were fearful of angering others and shrank from exposing themselves to notice in any way."

To summarize what was responsible for the boy's self-esteem, he said, "his treatment and achievements." To support these two things in their children the parents were interested in their welfare, concerned about their companions, available for discussion of their problems, and participated in joint activities that both enjoyed.

He described the parents as: ones who proved to be less permissive, set high standards of behavior, and were strict and consistent in the enforcement of the rules. Of course, their discipline was by no means abusive, but stern and sure.

It is important what you think about yourself and how you help develop that self-esteem in your children. How you relate to others depends to a large extent on how you feel about yourself.

If you see yourself as a failure, no good, not an achiever; or if you have negative thoughts about yourself and others reinforce those thoughts by saying, "You are always in trouble," or "You are a dummy," or "You can't do anything right;" or you think, "She does everything better than me," or "They only say that to be nice;" or you say, "I'm going to end it all and then they will be sorry," you are probably sufering from a low self-esteem.

Maxwell Maltz is *Psycho-Cybernetics*[2] said:

> "Self-image is the KEY to human personality and human behavior. Change the self-image and you change the personality and the behavior."

Bruce Narramore in *You're Someone Special*[3] said:

> "Our self-esteem is the source of our personal happiness or lack of it. It establishes the boundaries of our accomplishments and defines the limits of our fulfillments. If we think little of ourselves, we either accomplish little or drive ourselves unmercifully to disprove our negative self-evaluation. If we think, positively about ourselves, we are free to achieve our true potential."

It is important what you think about yourself and how you feel your spouse feels about you.

Rate Your Spouse's Acceptance

		NO	MID	YES
1.	I feel guilty when I ask for things or sometimes want my way.	3	2	1
2.	I am afraid of making mistakes around him/her.	3	2	1
3.	I feel it necessary to defind my actions when I'm with him/her.	3	2	1
4.	I am bothered by fear of feeling stupid or inadequate with him/her.	3	2	1
5.	Criticism from him/her hurts my feelings of worth.	3	2	1
6.	I feel free to show my weaknesses in front of him/her.	1	2	3
7.	I can care for myself in spite of his/her feeling for me.	1	2	3
8.	I am afraid to be myself with him/her.	3	2	1
9.	I feel free to express my needs to him/her.	1	2	3
10.	I find that I must give him/her reasons for my feelings.	3	2	1
11.	I can be negative or positive with him/her.	1	2	3
12.	My wants, dislikes and values are respected by him/her.	1	2	3
13.	I sometimes ask for my needs to be met.	1	2	3
14.	I can be inconsistent or illogical with him/her.	1	2	3
15.	I am afraid to show my fears to him/her.	3	2	1
16.	I am afraid to show tears in front of him/her.	3	2	1

SCORING: After you have responded to each statement, add up your score. The highest possible score is 48; the lowest score is 16. Remember, you are rating your spouse by saying how accepted YOU FEEL. The ratings are as follows:

40 - 48 strong feelings of acceptance
32 - 39 lack some feelings of acceptance
24 - 31 serious feelings of unacceptance
16 - 23 your communication needs lots of work

The Bible gives us a foundation for self-acceptance. From Genesis 1 to Revelation 22 the Bible stresses that God had placed a high value on each man. God said through the Bible writers:

> Genesis 1:26,27: *"Let Us make man in Our image, according to Our likeness; let them have dominion. . .over all the earth. . .So God created man in His own image."*

We are told that God made each of us in His own image.

> Psalm 8:5: *"For You have made him a little lower than the angels, And You have crowned him with glory and honor."*

You and I are crowned with glory and honor by God our father.

> Revelation 22:1-5: *"And he showed me a pure river of water of life, clear as crystal, proceeding from the throne of God and of the Lamb. In the middle of its street, and on either side of the river, was the tree of life, which bore twelve fruits. . .And there shall be no more curse. . .And there shall be no night there. . .for the Lord God gives them light. And they shall reign forever and ever."*

We will reign with God for eternity.

These verses and others give at least seven reasons why we should love ourselves.[4]

1. First, because **God created us in His image, our Royal heritage.** I believe this is a key to the foundation for a good self-esteem.

While attending a meeting of scholars, Thomas Carlyle was asked about the origin of man. He responded, "Gentlemen, you place man a little higher than the tadpole. I hold with the Psalmist, 'Thou hast made him a little lower than the angels.' "

This is the problem with human philosophies. Either man is an advanced animal, or he is the eternal creation of the living God! Our whole identity hinges on this point. Are we just another step in the evolutionary process, or are we the result of the creative genius of God? This is the bedrock of self-esteem!

We are created by the hand of God and in His image. Genesis 1:26. Just like a book reflects its author, so you and I reflect a portion of God's character.

- We are like Him in that we have a great intellectual capacity.
- We can use that information to make complex decisions.
- We also have the capacity of self-determination. We can make plans, forsee results, make choices that effect our future.
- We have a great creative ability. New inventions, great works of art, exploration of nature and space, all are part of our God nature.

But our God nature goes even deeper. We have a *moral nature*

43

which enables us to deal with spiritual and ethical matters. This moral nature was stamped into the life of every man and woman by God. We know God was pleased with His creation. He said, after looking at His creation, "It is very good." Genesis 1:31.

2. **The order of the creation.** God started with the heavens and the earth, formed the sun and moon, seas, fish and birds, beasts of the field, everything that grows. He said it was good.

But after finishing all this, something was missing. With all the grandeur of the universe, God still wanted man, who is the only creature who can share in the thoughts and feelings of God. Man is the apex of God's creation.

3. **Our Kingly calling.** God placed man in the garden and told him, "Be fruitful and multiply; fill the earth and subdue it; have dominion over the fish of the sea, over the birds of the air, and over every living thing that moves on the earth." Genesis 1:28.

One commentator said of this verse:

> "These words plainly declare the vocation of the human race is to RULE. Far from being something in conflict with God, cultural achievements are an essential attribute of the nobility of man as he possessed it in Paradise. Inventions, discoveries, the sciences and the arts, in short, the advance of the human mind are throughout the will of God. They are the "taking possession" of the earth by the royal human race."

God is pleased when we accomplish. He wants us to. He knows we can and expects us too. He is displeased if we don't use our talents.

Some people don't see this. They constantly talk of their plight in life. "We are poor, born that way and will always be poor, God made us that way."

Baloney! People are designed to achieve! You have the same capacity to accomplish as anyone else. It is your desire, and drive to achieve that makes the difference. God has given you the capacity to succeed, but it's up to you to use your ability.

4. **We are the "Salt of the earth."** God places a high value on man. Throughout the ministry of Jesus He affirms our value and importance to God. "You are the salt of the earth. . .You are the light of the world" Matthew 5:13,14. "Look at the birds of the air, for they neither sow nor reap nor gather into barns; yet your heavenly father feeds them. Are you not of much more value than they?" Matthew 6:26.

Over and over Jesus proclaims our value. Maybe the best picture of our value is seen in Jesus' prayer for us. As He faces the cross He prays to His father:

"I pray for them. I do not pray for the world but for those whom You have given Me, for they are Yours. And all Mine are Yours, and Yours are Mine, and I am glorified in them. Now I am no longer in the world, but these are in the world. . .keep through Your name those whom You have given Me, that they may be one as We are. . .And the glory which You gave Me I have given them, that they may be one just as We are one: . . .that they may be made perfect in one, and that the world may know that You have sent Me, and have loved them as You have loved Me." John 17:9-11,22,23.

Jesus is under tremendous pressure as He faces His death, but He wants us to be united with Him for eternity. He closes by telling us that God loves us as MUCH as He loves His own son. God loves me just as He loves Jesus. WOW! I can't fully undertand how much love that is, but I know the love I have for my girls and I know God's love is even greater.

5. The price of our redemption.

"Knowing that you were not redeemed with corruptible things, like silver or gold, from our aimless conduct received by tradition from your fathers, but with the precious blood of Christ, as a lamb without blemish and without spot." 1 Peter 1:18,19.

What a foundation for self-esteem! The purchase price tells us the value of an object. The price of my redemption was the blood of Jesus Christ. I must be very valuable to God! Christ didn't die for the animal kingdom or the vegetable kingdom, as valuable as they are, but for YOU and ME!

"You were bought at a price. . ." 1 Corinthians 6:20. What a sense of value and worth that knowledge brings to me. As a result:

1. **I have security.** "There is therefore now NO condemnation to those who are in Christ." Romans 8:1. I have forgiveness. I don't have to carry around all the guilt I may feel for past sins and mistakes, or be ashamed for past sins. They are forgiven because of Jesus and His grace given to me and all the world, and my obedient response to it.

Self-esteem helps you overcome feelings of guilt. Guilt keeps you in constant fear of being rejected, or feeling that you need to be punished in some way for the wrongs you have done. Guilt comes about when you don't meet up to your expectations of yourself, and it robs you of any sense of accomplishment.

One young girl committed a sin that caused her to be overwhelmed by guilt. She felt the sin was so great that even God could not forgive her. As a result, she did not love herself and felt she was unworthy of the love of anyone else. It was guilt that was destroying her life.

45

Finally, a friend led her to the scripture, "There is therefore now no condemnation to those who are in Christ." Romans 8:1. "If we confess our sins, He is faithful and just, to forgive us our sins. . ." 1 John 1:9. After some discussion she let Jesus remove that guilt from her life. She was made whole by her faith, prayer, repentance, and baptism in Christ. Acts 2:38. You have got to get rid of your guilt.

2. I have significance.

"You are a chosen generation, a royal priesthood, a holy nation, His own special people, that you may proclaim the praise of Him who called you out of darkness into His marvelous light." 1 Peter 2:9.

I am somebody! I am somebody! I am a child of God, a holy person, a royal priest, a people of God.

To see yourself in that light, to know that God feels that way about you, you can't help but feel good and important. His power will supply your needs!

3. I am competent.

"For God has not given us a spirit of fear, but of power and of love and of a sound mind." 2 Timothy 1:7. *"I can do all things through Christ who strengthens me."* Philippians 4:13.

I CAN DO! I can accomplish anything, with God's help. Why? Because as a Christian I have the power of God working in me.

The more I study the Bible, the more I see that every person is entitled to an attitude of self-acceptance, self-love, and self-worth. The Bible clearly teaches that we should love ourselves, not in an arrogant fashion, but in humility.

- We are created in God's image.
- We are creatures of value and worth.
- We were so important that Christ died to save us from sin and eternal death.

Let me apply these principles, and suggest some practical ways to help you build self-worth in yourself and others.

1. Show your loved ones that they are worthwhile by the way you honor and respect them.
- If you think someone is great, tell them.
- Husbands tell your wives, wives tell your husbands, children tell your parents, parents tell your children, "You are great and I love you!"
- Even if they aren't great, tell them anyway. If you say it they will believe it, and it will help produce in them what you want them to be.

2. Be sensitive to and protect the feelings of others. Everyone has feelings. If you call someone a LOUSE, he will be hurt and act like a LOUSE. Sensitivity is the key. Practice the Golden Rule and support others as you want others to support you.

3. Be responsive to others. Sometimes we get so wrapped up in what we are doing that we ignore others.

My youngest daughter can watch T.V. with such intensity that you have to literally break her vision of the T.V. before you can get her attention to tell her something.

I am afraid that many men let job pressures and social activities dominate their time and have nothing left for their wives and family. We have got to listen to each other - learn to communicate.

4. Be open about our faults. Some are afraid to tell their spouse about a fault. Maybe they are afraid of being rejected by their mate. But when you communicate to your partner freely and honestly about your problems, bare yourself to the other person, then they can bare themselves to you. The walls will come down and you can talk openly with each other.

5. Let the other person know that in your eyes they are a beautiful person, no matter what they have done or will do. Beauty is in the eye of the beholder. Don't worry about what other people think of that person.

Paul rebuked the Corinthians for not praising and honoring those members of the church that seemed less important. Paul said all are important to God and His people. 1 Corinthians 12:22-24.

6. Let the other person know you believe in them. You have faith in them, and have confidence in what they will do.

God became angry with Moses for his lack of confidence in his ability to do the work God has chosen him to do. Moses made excuses about his ability and God rebuked him for his excuses. Exodus 4:10-14.

In his book *Psycho Cybernetics,* Dr. Maltz, a plastic surgeon, told some observations he had made about a few of his patients after they had disfiguring scars removed.

> "Some patients show no change in personality after surgery. In most cases a person who had a conspicuously ugly face corrected by surgery experienced an almost immediate (within 21 days) rise in self-esteem, and self-confidence. But in some cases, the patient continues to feel inadequate and experiences feelings of inferiority. In short, these "failures" continue to feel, act, and behave just as if they still have an ugly face."

I believe Dr. Maltz is right in his observation. You can fix up the outside and make it beautiful, but it's what is on the inside that counts. How you feel about yourself that will help you make your life and your marriage a success.

Questions

1. "How you relate to others depends to a large extent on how you feel about yourself." Is this statement true or false. Why?

2. Give some suggestions about how you build self-esteem in your own life. How do you build self-esteem in your spouse and family?

3. Some people have said that self-esteem is not necessary and not a characteristic of a Christian. Do you agree with that statement? If not, why?

4. What things can you do to help your spouse feel accepted by you? What things does your spouse do that make you feel accepted by him/her?

[1]Stanley Coopersmith, "Self-Respect in Children," *Scientific American*, Feb., 1968.
[2]Maxwell Maltz, *Psycho-Cybernetics*, New York: Essandess.
[3]Bruce Narramore, *You're Somebody Special*, Grand Rapids, Michigan: Zondervan, 1978. Used by permission.
[4]Ibid.

CHAPTER 6

The Bible Principle Of Submission

In the beginning when God had created the earth and all that was in it, He looked down on a lonely Adam and said, "It is not good that man should be alone; I will make him a helper comparable to him." Genesis 2:18. God then brought all the beasts of the earth before Adam. He saw the lion playing with the lioness, and all the creatures seems to have a companion just right for them. But for Adam, there was not found a helper.

So God caused a deep sleep to fall on Adam, and from his side God took a rib and fashioned a woman. Eve, of all the creations on the earth, met the needs of Adam's body, his heart, and his mind. She was a helper FIT for him in every way.

God could have created her out of the dust, as He did Adam, but I believe God wanted Adam to know how greatly he needed Eve. He wanted him to know that she was actually a part of his body - as his heart or brain. He wanted them both to know they were actually, physically, ONE flesh in the deepest and holiest sense of the word. And that same oneness is created even today when a man and woman stand before God and take one another, leaving all others, and become one flesh.

It was a great day. Man had his companion, friend, lover, and compassionate helper.

But one dark day came, the darkest day of all, even above the crucifixion, because it produced the crucifixion. Eve listened to the serpent in the garden. She believed Satan's lie. She ate of the forbidden fruit and gave it to her husband. Together they inherited not what Satan promised, but the curse of death.

When God walked through the garden in the cool of that somber day, He found two creatures hiding in the nakedness of their sin. In a voice that struck dread in the heart of the first woman, God said, "Your desire shall be for your husband, And HE WILL RULE OVER YOU." Genesis 3:16.

Then the great God of heaven and earth in love and compassion clothed their nakedness and began His great plan to bring about the salvation of His children.

The command God uttered that day to the woman still stands today! There are some reasons for this command and I believe when we understand WHY God requires a wife to submit to her husband, it makes this command easier to bear.

1. **God's perfect creation required order.**[1] God has set up a chain of command in the family and it required the husband to be in authority over the woman.

> "Let a woman learn in silence with all submission. And I do not permit a woman to teach or to have authority over a man, But to be in silence. For Adam was formed first, then Eve."
> 1 Timothy 2:12,13.

The rest of the chain of authority, or command, is given in 1 Corinthians 11:3, "The head of every man is Christ, the head of woman is man, and the head of Christ is God." The chain of authority is: God, Christ, man and woman.

Christ our Lord is in subjection to God, the father. At one time He was equal with the father, but because of His love for lost man, He humbled Himself to God, became a man, and died for our sins. Philippians 2:5-8. "Though He was a son, yet He learned obedience by the things which He suffered." Hebrews 5:8. 'I do not seek my own will but the will of the Father who sent Me." John 5:30. Even when Christ has conquered all the forces of evil, He will then submit Himself to God! Even when Christ has conquered all the forces of evil, He will then submit Himself to God! "When all things are made, (subject to Him), then the son Himself will also be subject to Him who put all things under Him, that God may be all in all." 1 Corinthians 15:28.

Jesus, the great God and Savior of the world, submitted Himself to God, the father. He took His place in the chain of authority.

The point is, there is NO SHAME, or dishonor for a woman to be under the authority of her husband, if the Lord Jesus Himself submitted to the authority of His father. Position in the chain of authority has nothing to do with the individual's worth to God or value in this life. Position is not determined by one's importance. A woman is subject to her husband, but she can go straight to God in prayer and ask anything she needs or desires, and God will answer her prayers as He does all mankind. "There is neither Jew nor Greek, there is neither slave nor free, there is neither male nor female; for you are all one in Christ Jesus." Galatians 3:28.

Also, a man should not be over inflated with pride because he stands before the woman in the chain of command.

"Nevertheless, neither is man independent of woman, nor woman independent of man, in the Lord. For as the woman was from the man, even so the man also is through the woman; but all things are from God." 1 Corinthians 11:11,12.

There is no place for boasting by man or woman. Each has a blessing and unique responsibility in the marriage relationship that only they can fulfill and can not happily exist without it.

God made man the provider for the home. He is to be the high priest, or spiritual leader for his wife and children. He has the responsibility for his children to guide them, nurture them and direct them in the ways of God for a happy life. Ephesians 6:1-4.

In God's plan, He made a woman to be the keeper of the home. Her purpose is to make it a haven for the family, to nourish the children. A woman's body is fashioned for being a wife and mother. Why do some feel that is degrading? Her body is shaped to bear children. Never a month goes by that she is not reminded of that basic creative function. Her body is shaped to be the lover of her husband.

A woman is different from a man! She is different in her body, in her interest, in her thinking, in her abilities. I didn't say INFERIOR, but DIFFERENT!

I really believe that a wife can find her greatest sense of fulfillment in life, or satisfaction in life, when she is secure in the knowledge of her womanhood and its rightness, and building a happy home for herself, her husband, and her children.

2. **Woman's nature requires her obedience.** The truth is seen in Paul's statement to Timothy.

"And Adam was not deceived, but the woman being deceived, fell into transgression. Nevertheless she will be saved in childbearing if they continue in faith, love and holiness, with self-control." 1 Timothy 2:14,15.

She was the one who was desirous of the fruit, and got her husband to eat of it. She was the one that was deceived by Satan. Adam was not. This really pictures something for us about the woman and spiritual leadership.

Normally, we picture the woman as the more spiritually-minded person in the family. But the truth is, according to scripture, the op-

51

posite is true. Women are more often led into spiritual error than men. Why? I don't know, unless maybe it is her emotional or intuitive thinking. Maybe that is the reason God commanded her not to have authority over the man, so she can be protected (so to speak) from false teachers and their false doctrine.

There are all kinds of examples of this thought in scripture. The most familiar is Rebekah's conspiracy against Isaac to get his blessing for her favorite son, Jacob. Genesis 27. She went to great lengths to fool Isaac. She wanted the patriarchal blessing to go to her favorite son. The problems she caused by her deception have not only the brothers fighting, but even the great nations that are their descendants. The deception was unnecessary because God had already told her before the twins' birth that the older son would serve the younger (Genesis 25:23), but she did it anyway. How sad deception is, and how destructive it can be.

But when a wife starts trying to be the leader in spiritual affairs of the home, things go wrong. So her nature requires obedience.

3. **Scripture demands obedience.** Many scriptures demand the submission of the wife to her husband. Paul pictures the relationship between Christ and the church as that of the husband to his wife. Ephesians 5:22-23. He said,

"As Christ also loved the church and gave Himself up for it, that He might sanctify and cleanse it with the washing of water by the word, that He might present it to Himself a glorious church, not having spot or wrinkle or any such thing, but that it should be holy and without blemish." verses 25-27.

Paul said, "So, husbands ought to love their own wives as their own bodies." v. 28.

Of the wife Paul said, "Wives, submit to your husbands, as to the Lord. For the husband is head of the wife, as also Christ is head of the church;" v. 22. Further he says, ". . .Let the wife see that she respects her husband." v. 33. The submission the wife shows to her husband is a picture of how the church is to submit to the Lord Jesus Christ.

Other verses say, "Wives, submit to your own husbands, as is fitting in the Lord." Colossians 3:18.

"The older women. . .admonish the younger women to love their husbands, to love their children, to be discreet, chaste, homemakers, good, obedient to their own husbands, that the word of God may not be blasphemed." Titus 2:3-5, 1 Peter 3:1,5,6.

Many women will read verses like these in the New Testament that teach submission to the husband and reject them. Why? Don't they want to please God by submitting to His word? I hope so. But some have given these reasons as to why they don't submit:

1. "It doesn't fit in with my idea of what marriage should be."
2. "I don't want to think that I'm not equal with my husband."
3. "It was only meant for the illiterate women of the Old and New Testament times."
4. "Women are intelligent beings and should be able to stand on their own two feet."
5. "If it means being a doormat, I don't want any part of it."
6. "I'm not about to let any man, even my husband, tell me how to run my life."
7. "I want to be submissive, but I don't know how, or understand what it means."
8. "I've tried it off and on, but haven't found it to be very joyful, so I've gone back to my old ways."
9. "The only person I have to be submissive to is God."
10. "We would never make it if I didn't run this household."

God didn't create woman to be the dominant partner in the marriage. Nowhere in scripture do we find this indicated. Paul said of the Christian wife to SUBMIT to her husband. "You are doing what is right, and fitting, and your proper duty in the Lord." Colossians 3:18, (Amplified Bible).

In all these verses, God tells the husband to LOVE his wife, but He always first says, "wives be submissive." Submission is the one thing that makes the wife more lovable, and able to accept the love of her husband.

Again, some excuse their non-submission by saying, "But, I don't always agree with my husband;" or "We wouldn't be where we are today if I didn't stand my ground once in a while;" or "You mean I never get to speak my piece?" or "What if he asks me to do something I don't want to do?"

These statements show that many women don't understand what submission is, and how the husband is to act in the family.

First, the husband's leadership is not autocractic. He doesn't command and the wife obeys. His is a servant leadership. He leads his family by being the greatest servant in the family. He puts their needs and feelings before his own because of his love for them.

Second, when the wife disagrees with her husband, she should tell him how she feels, but in a way that doesn't challenge his God-given authority. Many times the tone of voice, or the words used, or the way she says it, implies that she is trying to take his authority away and cast his decision aside.

Third, I believe scripture teaches that God holds the man responsible for what happens in the family. A wife can commit sin and do sinful things that will cause her to be lost; she is responsible for her personal sin. But, when it comes to the family and decisions that affect the spirituality of the family, the man is accountable to God!

One example is Sarai in Genesis 12:11-13. Abram asked Sarai to lie about their relationship as husband and wife. Her heart was right in the matter and God held Abram responsible for what went wrong, as did Pharaoh. v. 18.

If you choose when to obey your husband, you are not submitting to him at all. You are simply doing your own will and sometimes it just happens to coincide with his wishes.

I do believe there are exceptions to this rule. One is when the husband asks you to go against God's will. God's will is to be first, even before a husband's will. Matthew 10:32-39. I believe that by a wife's submission to God, and her husband, the beauty of that life of submission will win that unbelieving husband to Christ. 1 Peter 3:1-6.

One husband said, "Your being submissive to me scares me to death. Before, if I asked you to do something you didn't agree with, you objected in no uncertain terms, or just didn't do it. Now that you have decided to be fully submissive, I am very careful about what I ask you to do."

I believe the above statement to be the result of Biblical submission. The responsibility for the actions of the family weights heavily on the husband. He is very careful and very considerate of the wife's needs when he knows that she will follow his leadership.

Let me warn you about inconsistency in submission. If a wife is not consistent in her submission, the husband will think that she is using it to get her way in a certain matter and will not trust her submission. You have got to be consistent.

Wives, do you remember that day when you first realized how much you loved that man you married? Do you remember that you felt if you had him you could put your hand in his and go anywhere in the world without fear? You were just happy to be together.

Well, he is still that same man, basically. Can you not love him enough, trust him enough, and trust God enough to give back to him that simple faith in his ability to love you and make the decisions that are for your benefit and for your happiness? Sure, he has made mistakes, everyone does, but with your input and love and spirit of support, and by praying together he can make those decisions that will be for your happiness.

It's all there, a marvelous world of love, trust, and usefulness to God and your husband. It's all waiting for the wife to claim through the simple act of submission.

Questions

1. In God's chain of authority for the family, woman is after man. Why did God place woman under man's authority? Does this mean she is inferior to man?

2. In scripture the man and woman are given different responsibilities in the home. Discuss those responsibilities and why they are different.

3. If you choose when you will submit to your husband's authority are your really submitting to it at all? Why?

4. What responsibility does the man have to his wife to help her practice submission to his authority? How can he help her to submit?

¹From the book, **Me? Obey Him?** by Elizabeth Rice Handford, Sword of The Lord Publishers; used by permission.

CHAPTER 7

Communication - The Key To A Marriage

G ood communication in the family between husbands and wives, and parents and children is a key to having an effective relationship.

Without it, any couple will drift apart. Husbands and wives should talk and discuss their goals, judge values, and analyze ambitions with complete and open integrity.

If they don't, their marriage will never be the happy marriage it could be.

Dr. David Mace, past president of the American Association of Marriage Counselors, has said, "Poor communication is the main problem in 86% of all troubled marriages."[1]

What then is communication? It is defined by Norman Wright as:

"The process of both verbal and non-verbal sharing in such a way that one's message can be accepted and understood by another. It is the process of transmitting and receiving feelings, attitudes, facts, and beliefs that transpire between living beings."[2]

From this definition we can see why it is not only important WHAT we say, but HOW we say it. Scripture says we must learn to "speak the truth in love." Ephesians 4:15.

In the list below, which one of the items gives you the most trouble in your communication with your spouse?

1. Talking before you think.
2. Getting angry too quickly.

3. Overreacting in the situation.
4. Sharing your feelings.
5. Clouding the real issue.
6. Your attitude.

In the classes that Judy and I have conducted on marriage, we find the answers given most often reflect two things.

1. Overreacting in the situation.
2. Inability to share your feelings with another.

Overreacting is when the person you are talking with all of a sudden blows his stack for no apparent reason. It is a childish response. Sometimes it is produced by a person's lack of control over his temper.

The person who is **unable to open up with others,** to share his feelings as to what he really thinks or feels, this inability is sometimes produced by fear. The fear may be fear of rejection, fear that others will make fun of him, or fear that his love will not be accepted.

Both are tremendous barriers to effective communication in the family, between friends, and in the church.

I am thankful to God that the writer, James, gives us an answer to deal with BOTH of these problems.

"Let every man be swift to HEAR (listen), slow to SPEAK (think before you speak), and slow to WRATH (practice self-control)." James 1:19.

The point - the good communicator will listen carefully to what is said and be very careful about his response. He doesn't overreact to the situation, or fly off-the-handle, but instead he thinks about the effect his words and tone of voice will have on the other person.

Good listening is not a skill you are born with, but something everyone can develop after hours of practice and training. Basically in listening, you are giving a person your full and undivided attention as he expresses to you his inner feelings and experiences, by his words and actions. There are three elements involved in listening:

1. It means that when another person is talking you are not thinking about what you are going to say when he stops talking.

Have you ever talked with a person that you just could not get through to? Every time you said something, his response was on a different question or was so evasive that you wondered if he even heard the question. He is not listening!

2. Listening is complete acceptance, without judgment, of what is said or how it is said. This does not mean you agree with everything that is said, but for the moment you are going to listen and try to understand what the other person is saying without reaction.

Some people are shocked by what they hear. They judge a person immediately by their reaction. We think a man is a drunkard when he asks a question about drinking. A father thinks his son is a drug addict if he asks a question about drugs. Don't judge - listen!

3. Listening means that you can restate accurately both the CONTENT, and the FEELINGS of the message that was sent to you.

Gossip and slander are started by hearing only half truths. "The ear that hears the reproof of life will abide among the wise." Proverbs 15:31. It is wise to listen!

"He who answers a matter before he hears it, it is FOLLY and SHAME to him." Proverbs 18:13.

In many marriages, communication is either the problem or it becomes the dumping ground for all the other problem areas. I have seen situations where both the husband and the wife had good feelings about each other, but because they were unable to communicate those good feelings, they mis-communicated. The wife's feelings were hurt and the husband's feelings neglected, so conflict ensued.

I believe that married couples are always communicating. The problem is the KIND of messages they are sending are not the ones they want to send.

John Powell in his book, **Why Am I Afraid To Tell You Who I Am?**[3], suggests five levels of conversation:

Level 5 - Cliche conversation. This type of communication is safe and shallow. "How's the weather?" "How are you?" No personal involvement.

Level 4 - Reporting the facts about others. At this level we tell others what someone else has said or done, but we offer no personal opinions about these facts.

Level 3 - My ideas and judgments. Real communication begins here. The person is willing to risk sharing some of his own ideas or judgments. He is still cautious and if what he says is rejected or made fun of, he will retreat.

Level 2 - My feelings or emotions. The person communicating at this level is really sharing himself. He states his feelings about facts, ideas, and judgments. His inner feelings are revealed.

Level 1 - Peak communication. This is complete emotional and truthful communication. It knows no holding back, it is total honesty.

A relationship as husband and wife, or parent and child, or even close friends needs level one communication if it is to produce the closeness and openness you want.

It is very important that both partners be able to communicate on level one. I believe it is easy to see the result of level one communication. A relationship that is completely open and honest, where both partners don't hold back their feelings, but communicate in LOVE, is destined to be a success. If both partners will receive the messages honestly and act on them.

I realize some people are afraid of this type of communication. They feel the need to keep some deception present in their marriage, and build their relationship on fantasies. But a relationship built on fantasies only produces frustration and hurt in the days to come.

God's word says, "Speak the truth in love. . ." Ephesians 4:15. "Putting away, lying, each one speak truth with his neighbor, for we are members of one another." verse 25. "He who would love life, And see good days, Let him refrain his tongue from evil, And his lips from speaking guile." 1 Peter 3:10. The result of truthful communication is to have good days and love life!

"A good man out of the good treasure of his heart brings forth good. . .For out of the abundance of the heart his mouth speaks." Luke 6:45. What major factor determines the quality of our speech? Jesus says it is our HEART! If it is open, honest, truthful, and good, good things will come out of our mouth. When you possess that kind of heart, you can't help but have level one communication.

Here are eight ways you can improve your communication skills:

1. **Be knowledgeable of the other person.** "Dwell with them with understandings, giving honor to the wife." 1 Peter 3:7. The word UNDERSTANDING means the husband will be SENSITIVE and CONSIDERATE of his wife. These two things require that he have a knowledge of her and that requires time. Time when the two are alone and share with each other their feelings openly and honestly.

2. **Be loving of her.** Anyone can carry on a beautiful relationship when the spouse does all the right things. But, when things begin to break down, it's another matter. Unconditional love is required. It takes a lot of love to forgive someone who has abused you with his words or physically, but as a Christian Jesus tells us to love in that fashion. 1 Corinthians 13:4-8. This love says, "I love you whether I feel like it or not." If you act in love, these actions will force you and your spouse to see the course that should be followed. This is *agape* love - unconditional love.

3. **Be transparent or open to each other.** To me this is one of the most important points in good communication. It is foolish to share your innermost thoughts in casual conversation, but it is a greater tragedy NOT to share them with the person you have chosen to spend the rest of your life with. Christians have the added dimension of being able to look deeper and more profoundly into each other because of the spirit of God. It enables us to forgive any sin or ugliness we might find there. "To deeply love, is to deeply know."

4. **Be trustworthy.** There is no room for suspicion or jealousy in

marriage. Trust is a characteristic of unconditional love. 1 Corinthians 13:4.

5. **Be sensitive.** It is the feeling level of communication. Be aware of the feelings of the other person. I guess men are the biggest offenders in this area.

6. **Be an effective communicator.** I understand what I am saying so I assume that others will hear my words exactly as I do. But they don't.

What do I mean when I say, "A.S.U." From around here it means, Arkansas State University, or Alabama State University. But if you are from out West, it could mean Arizona State University.

There are many examples of words like this that have different meanings in different places, so make sure the other person understands what you mean. Maybe even define your words.

7. **Be an active listener.** What I mean is give the other person your full attention. Center in on the words, tone, and feelings expressed. Also, listen for what is NOT SAID.

8. **Be prayerful.** By this I mean pray together about your marriage, your problems, your children, your goals, your understanding of each other, everything that effects your marriage. Nowhere else can you see the inner cares and thoughts of your spouse as when you pray to God about each other. You can lay before Him all the hurts and problems and He will help you with them.

Someone suggested these additional ways to help your communication:

1. Don't assume you know - ask!
2. Provide an open, permissive, accepting atmosphere.
3. Use compliments freely.
4. Pray for each other and together.
5. Be willing to disagree, but in a gentle way.
6. Concentrate on being a good listener.
7. Build up your mate's self-esteem.
8. Seek more to understand than to be understood.
9. When you are wrong or have sinned against your mate, admit it and ask for forgiveness.

All that I have said in this chapter will help you to improve your communication skills, but the key is whether or not you will put into practice all that you have learned. You have to take that first step and open the door to have the openness you want. No one else can do it for you.

ASSIGNMENT: Plan an evening where there are no interruptions - no TV, no phones, no children, just you and your spouse. Spend that time talking about what is on your heart. Start with some goals, or fears you have, and work up to what you need from each other. It may prove to be one of the most life changing evenings of your life.

How To Fight Fairly

Paul said, "Avoid foolish and ignorant disputes, knowing that they generate strife." 2 Timothy 2:23. Even though we don't feel our arguments are senseless, I believe Paul is right in his summation of many of the things we fight about in marriage. We need to settle the matter quickly (Matthew 5:25) so that we can center in on more important things.

Paul Faulkner has given these suggestions about how to argue fairly.[4]

1. **Clarify the issue.** Make sure you know what it is you are arguing about.

2. **Repeat their words.** Check out your assumption. Sometimes a person doesn't say what he means.

3. **Choose the right time.** When you argue before you go to bed (12 o'clock) both are tired and not able to think as they should.

4. **Look before you leap.** If the goal is not worth the risk, concede before you start.

5. **Resolve to resolve.** Often we argue about one thing and all the unresolved arguments of the past come up. Finish it, come to a conclusion before you go to another.

6. **Attack the problem, not the person.** When you are losing the argument, don't resort to mud-throwing. It is always counterproductive.

7. **Hold hands.** Silly, but it works. It is hard to argue with someone who is holding your hand and looking you in the eye.

Questions On Chapter 7

1. Which of these items gives you the most problems in communicating? (a) Talking before you think, (b) Getting angry too quickly, (c) Overreacting to a situation, (d) Sharing your feelings, (e) Clouding the real issue, (f) Your attitude.

2. What do you feel is the greatest barrier to effective listening?

3. Can level one communication really be achieved?

4. What are some suggestions you have to improve communication skills in your family?

[1]David Mace, "Marriage As Relationship-In Depth," Edited by H.L. Silverman, **Marital Therapy,** Springfield, Illinois: Thomas, 1972.

[2]Norman Wright, **Communication, Key To Your Marriage,** Ventura, California: Gospel Light Publications.

[3]John Powell, **Why Am I Afraid To Tell You Who I Am?,** Valencia, California: Tabor Publishing, 1978. Used by permission.

[4]Paul Faulkner and Carl Brecheen, **What Every Family Needs,** Austin, Texas: Sweet Publishing Company, 1979.

Are You Communicating?

To test communication between you and your spouse, circle the answers that you feel best represent your level of communication. Then add up the numbers and compare your score to the table below. Be honest in your answers!

	Usually/	Some-times/	Seldom/	Never
1. Do you and your spouse discuss the manner in which the family income should be spent?	3	2	1	0
2. Does your spouse discuss his/her work and interest with you?	3	2	1	0
3. Do you have a tendency to keep your feelings to yourself?	0	1	2	3
4. Is your spouse's tone of voice irritating?	0	1	2	3
5. Are your mealtime conversations easy and pleasant?	3	2	1	0
6. Is it necessary to keep after your spouse about his/her faults?	0	1	2	3
7. Does your spouse seem to understand your feelings?	3	2	1	0
8. Does your spouse nag you?	0	1	2	3
9. Does your spouse listen to what you have to say?	3	2	1	0
10. Does your spouse say nice things to you/pay you compliments?	3	2	1	0
11. Is it hard to understand your spouse's feelings and attitudes?	0	1	2	3
12. Is your spouse affectionate toward you?	3	2	1	0
13. Does your spouse let you finish talking before responding to what you are saying?	3	2	1	0
14. Do you and your spouse remain silent for long periods of time when you are angry with one another?	0	1	2	3
15. Does your spouse allow you to pursue your own interests and activities even if they are different to his/hers?	3	2	1	0
16. Does your spouse try to lift your spirits when you are depressed/discouraged?	3	2	1	0
17. Do you fail to express disagreement with your spouse because you are afraid he/she will get angry?	0	1	2	3
18. Does your spouse complain that you don't understand him/her?	0	1	2	3
19. Do you let your spouse know when you're displeased with him/her?	3	2	1	0
20. Do you feel your spouse says one thing but really means another?	0	1	2	3
21. Do you help your spouse understand you by saying how you think, feel, and believe?	3	2	1	0
22. Do you and your spouse find it hard to disagree with one another without losing your tempers?	0	1	2	3
23. Do the two of you argue a lot over money?	0	1	2	3
24. When a problem arises that needs to be solved, are you and your spouse able to discuss it				

	together (In a calm manner)?	3	2	1	0
25.	Is it difficult to express your true feelings to your spouse?	0	1	2	3
26.	Does your spouse offer occupation, encouragement and emotional support in your role as wife/husband?	3	2	1	0
27.	Do you and your spouse engage in outside interests and activities together?	3	2	1	0
28.	Does your spouse let you know you are important to him/her?	3	2	1	0
29.	Is it easier to confide in a friend rather than your spouse?	0	1	2	3
30.	Does your spouse sulk or pout very much?	0	1	2	3
31.	Do you discuss intimate matters with your spouse?	3	2	1	0
32.	Do you discuss personal problems with each other?	3	2	1	0
33.	Do you talk over pleasant things that happen during the day?	3	2	1	0
34.	Do you hesitate to discuss certain things with your spouse because you are afraid he/she might hurt your feelings?	0	1	2	3
35.	Do the two of you ever sit down just to talk things over?	3	2	1	0

Add up the source for each answer and compare your total score to the chart. If your score indicates you have a problem with communication, please get some help today!

105-90 - Excellent Communication.   **89-70** - Good Communication.
  69-50 - Needs some work.   **49- 0** - You have a big problem!

CHAPTER 8

They Became One Flesh (Commitment)

A s they walked through the revolving doors and stood outside, they stopped and faced each other.

Janet said, "Honey, it's the same old story. They just don't think it will work."

Jack quickly replied, "But Janet, it will work regardless of what they all say. We love each other and we will make it work."

They stood there, looking into each other's eyes, then turned and began walking down the street to their car.

A decision had to be made and it would not be easy. Jack was from an affluent family and since his birth had been given whatever his heart desired and more. Janet's background was just the opposite. A broken home, a mother who worked, little money, few opportunities, life was a challenge just to survive.

After their accidental meeting in a restaurant where Janet was a waitress, there followed many memorable moments - movies, concerts, parties, outings. Finally Jack asked the question, "Will you marry me?"

For Janet, the whole experience had been filled with questions. "Why me? A man like Jack, what does he see in me?"

After much thought, Janet responded, "Jack, it just won't work. It just won't work. Your parents will be displeased, and mine will be suspicious. Anyway, there are just too many differences for us to have any possibility of success."

Nothing Jack could say would change her mind. Logic, reasoning, even arguments, they all failed. Finally, out of frustration, Jack suggested, "Let's go to a counselor. We will ask him to help and then decide, O.K.?"

Six appointments followed. They were filled with endless questions, tests, and discussion. Then the inevitable question was asked, "Will it succeed?" "Of course," the counselor explained, "the marriage could succeed, but the differences are substantial."

The stage was set for a decision. Logic, analysis, and past experience would dictate the impossibility of knowing for certain what the future might be.

Is there not some other ingredient which would help to solidify a relationship so that its future would be assured?

Jack began to talk as they left the counselor's office. "I love you, Janet! And no matter what the tests show, and the opinions are, I am willing to make a commitment to you. It will work! Others have scored well on the tests and then divorced. What's important is that you and I decide to make a commitment to each other."

Janet smiled at Jack. She reached over and took his hand, looked him in the eye and said, "We'd better go. If we are going to tell our parents, we had better get started."

In our age, we have the tendency to evaluate marriage, and the husband/wife relationship only from the lines of a graph or the score on a test. But the apparent weakness of these things is their accuracy. A purely objective test can't measure the degree of love, commitment and determination that two people have to make a marriage a success. But these are the ingredients that are most needed to make a marriage a success.

1. In God's design for marriage, woman was created to be a helpmate for man. Man was alone and she was to be his companion, to have fellowship with him, to share herself with man.

The word - alone - is the key. Because of man's loneliness, woman was designed. Every joy, every problem you have is made lighter when it is shared with someone else.

"Therefore a man shall LEAVE his father and mother and be JOINED to his wife, and they shall become ONE FLESH." Genesis 2:24. Three words are important in this verse that deal with commitment in marriage: Leave, Joined, and one flesh.

(1. LEAVE deals with maturity, independence. The youth is ready to make a way of its own.

(2. JOINED means welded together, glued together. Remember the illustration of the tree frog? This is important to commitment! The couple makes the commitment to love each other in times of joy or sorrow, in health or in sickness, whether they are rich or poor. This commitment is not just stated in the ceremony, but is to be lived every day

of their lives.

(3. ONE FLESH means the sexual union. Sex is a very important part of the commitment and foundation of a growing relationship no matter what age you are. Marriage is not just to have children. Marriage is for the fulfillment of this physical need.

"Marriage is honorable among all, and the bed undefiled; but fornicators and adulterers God will judge." Hebrews 13:4.

"Let the husband render to his wife the affection due her, and likewise also the wife to her husband. The wife does not have authority over her own body, but the husband does. And likewise the husband does not have authority over his own body, but the wife does. Do not deprive one another except with consent for a time, that you may give yourselves to fasting and prayer; and come together again so that Satan does not tempt you because of your lack of self-control." 1 Corinthians 7:3-5.

The sexual relation does create commitment and faithfulness in the marriage. There is an intimacy in the sexual relation that is not found in any other act. You are giving of yourself to your partner in the deepest and most intimate sense.

God designed the sexual relation - one flesh - to deepen, vitalize and enrich every aspect of the relationship. That is its purpose.

It allows one relationship in life to be unique and unlike any other. It is in this permanent, life-long relationship that the deepest of human needs (those that can only be met by another human) are satisfied. This is where commitment is found.

2. There are some barriers to commitment and achieving the happiness in marriage we want. In the studies I have seen, three barriers are always mentioned: Selfishness, pride and low self-esteem. I want to consider SELFISHNESS, which is the chief barrier to commitment.

Selfishness is defined as: "Caring unduly or supremely for oneself; regarding one's own comfort, advantage, etc., at the expense of others." (Websters).

Paul commanded Christians, "In lowliness of mind let each esteem others better than himself." Philippians 2:3. This verse does not mean that we are to think of ourselves as crude or a nobody, and everyone else as 100 times better than we are. That type of attitude builds low self-esteem. We are not to be selfish. We are to esteem or consider the needs of others. Think of others and their needs before you do for yourself.

This applies to the marriage! If I always demand my rights, my needs be fulfilled as I want before anyone else, then I am practicing selfishness. I am destroying the marriage because I am not considering my wife and her rights and needs first.

Men are the biggest offenders in this area of our relationships. Men are to lead in the family. (Ephesians 5). As a result, men fall into the trap of always doing everything in the family their way, to please themselves. All revolves around what Dad wants to do, or buy, or go, without regard to the needs of his wife and children. This is selfishness! Pure and simple selfishness!

The same thing can be said of some wives who dominate their husbands.

Remember the example of Haman in Esther 3:5. He commanded that everyone in the kingdom bow down to him. Mordecai would not. So Haman got mad and built a gallow to hang Mordecai. As it worked out, Haman himself was the one that was hung. This is the result of the childish attitude of jealousy as it is expressed when we don't get our way. SELFISHNESS!

Be mature enough in your marriage to see the needs of your spouse and supply them. One survey said that happy marriages have both partners who feel that the other partner is always doing more for them than they are for their partner, Amen!

3. The KEY to overcoming selfishness is to give of yourself to others - LOVE!

A preacher visited with a lady who had a beautiful garden. As they walked through the garden, she began to cut the roses right and left for the preacher to carry to his wife. The preacher, amazed, said, "You are robbing yourself of all this beauty." She replied, "Don't you know that the only way to make a rose bush bear is to cut the roses freely. The more you cut the more you get."

What a great lesson to learn. The more we give, the more we get in return! We fail to understand this principle about love. By giving love, we get love.

Listen to Jesus:

"Give, and it will be given to you: good measure, pressed down, shaken together, and running over will be put into your bosom. For with the same measure that you use, it will be measured back to you." Luke 6:38.

Jesus is saying that by giving we really learn to live, and become rich in this life.

Applying this principle to marriage - the husband who gives to his wife will receive more in return than he can give. If he gives love, concern, help and romance, he will receive from his wife love, concern, help and romance, even more than he gives because she sees his love demonstrated.

Scripture teaches that our lives are made more lovely, more beautiful, more worthwhile by the things we DO for others.

"Freely you have received, freely give." Matthew 10:8b.

"A generous soul will be made rich and he who waters will also be watered himself." Proverbs 11:25.

"It is more blessed to give than to receive." Acts 20:35b.

"He who sows sparingly will also reap sparingly, and he who sows bountifully will also reap bountifully." 2 Corinthians 9:6.

These verses all point to the fact that we are blessed when we give. We are the ones who receive the benefit when we give.

The poorest man in all the world is one who spends his entire life upon himself, absorbing everything possible, but giving nothing to help someone else with the burdens they have. He does nothing to bring happiness into the life of someone else. Scripture says he is not only poor on this earth, but poor in heavenly treasure also.

How is he poor? He might have money and material possessions, but treasure is not always measured in terms of money.

IN HIS MARRIAGE - he has lost the love of his wife and children.

IN HIS FRIENDSHIPS - he has lost the love of his friends, if he had any. Why? Because all his desires are for himself and his selfish gain. Oh, he might have friends that will stay and help him spend his money, but when the money is gone, so are they.

The antidote is LOVE, giving of ourselves to others. This is part of the commitment we make in marriage and true friendship.

Dwight Stevenson in his book, **Faith Takes A Name,**[1] tells of the time when Cortez, the Spanish explorer, disembarked his 500 conquistadors upon the eastern coast of Mexico. As soon as everyone was off the ships, Cortez ordered them to be burned. There was no turning back. It was either stand where they were, or go forward. There was no way they could retreat.

I view Marriage much in the same fashion. When Judy and I said our vows to each other, there was no thought of divorce. We committed our lives to each other for life. The key word is WE. Both of us made the commitment. Judy wants to be the best wife she can be, and I want to be the best husband I can be. So together we give to each other, we grow in our knowledge and understanding of each other, we change together, and as a result we succeed together. It is our COMMITMENT to each other that makes our marriage a success.

Alan Bryan tells this story.[2] A few years ago in one of the great churches in Houston, Texas, Alan was speaking. In the audience sat a sweet, gray haired lady, eyes sparkling, and a look of love in her eyes as she listened. She had been the wife of an elder, a fine man himself, but he had died just a few weeks before. Alan began to talk about expressing your love for your partner and the lady dropped her head and began to cry. After the service, she came up to Alan and said, "I guess you noticed that I began to cry today. I just couldn't help it. Let me tell you why. On the last night that my husband lived, he and I planned to go to another congregation to listen to a gospel preacher speaking that night. For some reason, we had gotten ready a little bit early, and he said to me, 'Hon, would you mind sitting down and letting me talk to you for just a few moments? There are a few things I want to say to you.' 'Darling, you have been a good wife to me; you've been a good help-meet, and you've loved me with every force of your being. I want you to know that I love you and appreciate you, and if something ever happens to me, I want you to know that I love you and love you very dearly.' "

She told Alan that after that, they got up and went out to the car and got in. They drove over to a nearby congregation. After he drove up into the parking lot and put on the brakes to stop the car, he slumped over the steering wheel. He had a sudden heart attack and was gone forever.

She said, "You know those few minutes that he spent just asking me to sit down there in the living room just to tell me how much he loved me and appreciated me are so precious. I would not take all the money in all the lands for the memories of those few minutes he spent saying, 'I love you and I appreciate you.' "

When I read of examples like this I cry, because I know that marriages can succeed and be happy. But it takes TWO people who love each other and are willing to commit their lives to each other, no matter what. That's what I want and I know you do too!

Questions

1. What advice would you give to Jack and Janet? Would you encourage them to get married?

2. Define COMMITMENT in marriage? What are some things you have done to help you with your commitment in marriage?

3. What do you consider to be the chief barrier to commitment in marriage? How can couples overcome that barrier?

4. In your marriage, what has been the chief barrier to your commitment? How did you and your spouse overcome that problem? Are you stronger as a result?

---

[1]Dwight Stevenson, **Faith Takes A Name,** New York: Harper, 1954.

[2]Alan Bryan, **Climbing Happiness Mountain,** Florence, Alabama: Success Dynamics, Inc., 1978.

CHAPTER 9

Sexuality And
The Christian

Sexuality is a very important part of the marriage relationship. For some just to discuss it in an open manner is very offensive, and considered in poor taste. They act as if sexuality is the product of a modern, wicked, pornographic mind. But the mind behind its creation is God. God made men and women sexual beings. Therefore, it is important for Christians as they consider marriage to understand God's concept for sex and mankind's need for sex.

To begin with I encourage you to take the SEX QUESTIONNAIRE at the end of this chapter. After you finish you will have a better understanding of how you rate in your sexual relationship in your marriage.

In the beginning, when God had created everything, He told man and woman to "Be fruitful, and multiply; fill the earth." Genesis 1:28. At the end of the chapter He said, "God saw everything that He had made, and indeed it was very good. . ." (v. 31). Sex in marriage is very good in God's sight.

In chapter two where the story of creation is retold in greater detail, it says God saw man's LONELINESS and decided to make a "helper comparable to him." Genesis 2:18. Before God created Eve, God presented to Adam every animal, but none was found suitable to be the partner of man. (v. 20). It is interesting to note God showed Adam that nothing but woman, who was designed for man, was suited to share his life. God blessed them and said, "Therefore a man shall leave his father and his mother and be joined to his wife, and they shall become one flesh." Genesis 2:24. The ONE FLESH says sex is a complete spiritual, emotional, and physical union of the two.

In chapter thirty-nine of Genesis, the story of Joseph and his refusal to commit adultery with Potiphar's wife (v. 9) teaches us that sexual advances outside of marriage are to be rejected. Joseph fled the situation leaving his garments in her hands. That is the only way I know to deal with lust. (Matthew 5:27-30).

Another passage that warns us about sex outside of marriage is Proverbs 5, 6, and 7. Solomon says in verses 15 - 19 of chapter 5, that sex is to be exciting, joyful, satisfying and captivating when it is done between a man and his wife. He says, "Drink water from your own cistern. . .Let them be only your own, And not for strangers with you." Solomon is emphasizing the importance of faithfulness in marriage.

Also, the whole book of Song Of Solomon (or Songs) is devoted to sex, romance and marriage. We will look at the book at the end of this chapter and consider some of the special assignments that Solomon gives to add romance and joy to our sexual relationships.

In the New Testament, Hebrews 13:4 says, "Marriage is honorable among all, and the bed undefiled; but fornicators and adulterers God will judge." The word translated BED in this verse could be translated "coitus," which is the Latin word for sexual intercourse. That's what it is talking about. So the inspired writer is saying that sex in marriage is HOLY, SACRED, GOD-GIVEN. Husbands and wives need to celebrate that fact!

Jesus exalted sex in marriage in Matthew 19:5,6. He reminds us of God's words in Genesis 2:24, "the two shall become one flesh."

Then, there is the passage that holds up sexual love as an ideal love.

"That each of you should know how to possess his own vessel in sanctification and honor, not in passion of lust, like the Gentiles who do not know God;" 1 Thessalonians 4:4,5.

Too many marriages today are based primarily on sexual attraction. The search for a marriage partner today seems to be more of a search for a sex partner, and not a life partner. Paul is trying to warn us.

In 1 Corinthians 7:2-5, Paul describes what sex can be like when it is based on a full and complete relationship. Paul recognizes that BOTH men and women have sexual needs. Basically he says it is a sin to refuse your mate's sexual advances. With that realization Christian marriages should have the best sexual relations.

"Nevertheless, because of sexual immorality, let each man have his own wife, and let each woman have her own husband. Let the husband render to his wife the affection due her, and likewise also the wife to her husband. The wife does not have

authority over her own body, but the husband does. And likewise the husband does not have authority over his own body, but the wife does. Do not deprive one another except with consent for a time, that you may give yourselves to fasting and prayer; and come together again so that Satan does not tempt you because of your lack of self-control." 1 Corinthians 7:2-5.

Notice three things: First, *Paul does not mention procreation* at all in this passage. Having babies is an important part of the sexual relation, but it is not the exclusive function. A moral relationship can't be achieved without regular and fairly frequent sexual satisfaction.

Second, Paul says that *each partner gives his own body to the other.* (v. 4). Such a gift is an extremely important gift and trust, and is never to be abused, but accepted in love with care. Neither partner rules over his own body, but has given that privilege to the partner. This is so very important to accept!

Third, Paul said, *"do not deprive one another."* (v. 5). What a strong, all-encompassing command. The King James Version uses the word - "defraud." Fraud is a sin, because you are stealing what belongs to someone else. Sexual satisfaction is so important in marriage that the inspired writer is trying to make it as plain as he can. Each partner is obligated by scripture to give of himself to his spouse.

What do other writers have to say about sex? Dr. Ed Wheat has said, "If you do what comes naturally in love-making, almost every time you will be wrong."[1] A sexual relationship that is characterized by sexual immorality, impurity, debauchery, hatred, discord, jealousy, fits of rage, selfishness, envy, drunkenness, and orgies will rob a couple of the sexual joy and eternal joy that God intended. All of these characteristics are WORKS OF THE FLESH - Galatians 5:19-21.

If couples are full of the spirit of God, they will have ever-increasing joy in their sexual relationship. It will be characterized by: love, joy, peace, patience, kindness, goodness, faithfulness, gentleness, and self-control. Galatians 5:22-24. Obviously, these characteristics will produce a more satisfying sexual relationship for both partners.

Current research also verifies this. A sociologist named *Sorocon* has found that husbands and wives who pray together are twice as likely to report a happy sex life. In addition, Redbook magazine's survey of 100,000 women showed that sexual satisfaction is significantly related to religious belief. "With notable consistency, the greater the intensity of a woman's religious convictions, the likelier she is to be highly satisfied with the sexual pleasures of marriage."[2]

Tim LaHaye, in his book, **The Act of Marriage,** lists nine good suggestions for husbands and wives that will help create in their spouse a wholesome appetite for lovemaking.[3]

FOR HUSBANDS:

1. **Learn as much as you can.** There are all kinds of tapes and books available on the subject that have a Christian perspective. I encourage you to read and study them. For the couple, it would be good to read or listen together and then discuss the subjects mentioned. Things that before were too personal or difficult to discuss, could be brought up at that time.

2. **Practice self-control.** The sex needs of a man can be satisfied in a matter of seconds, but the wife's needs cannot. Most men who accuse their wives of being frigid because she never reaches an orgasm are often the problem themselves. The solution is for the man to learn self-control and patience in the sexual relation and strive for the wife's satisfaction.

3. **Concentrate on your wife's satisfaction.** A wise husband will make his wife's satisfaction early in marriage a major priority, so they both can benefit from her knowledge. Books like *Masters and Johnson* "Human Sexual Response," and *Tim LaHaye's* book already mentioned can be great helps to any couple.

4. **Remember what arouses a woman.** The sight of a man's wife getting ready for bed is enough to excite the husband. But the wife responds to romance, soft loving words, the tender touch, etc. The husband has to put his wife first if he is desirous of an excited response. The key words are: TALKING AND TOUCHING.

5. **Protect her privacy.** Men are inclined to be sex braggers. Many a man has spoiled a beautiful relationship by revealing private secrets to his buddies. Hold her confidence.

6. **Beware of offensive odors.** Some have a bigger problem with this than others, but there is little excuse today for bad breath, body odor, or any other offensive smells.

7. **Don't rush lovemaking.** There is a place for quick sex, but as a rule couples need to take time for loveplay. Loveplay is a major key to the feminine response.

8. **Communicate freely.** It is difficult for couples to talk freely about sex. One engineer married to a school teacher wife reported, "My wife, after all these years, still doesn't know what turns me on." When asked if he had told her, he replied, "No, I find it embarrassing to talk about sex." How can she know if he doesn't tell her? How can he know if she doesn't tell him? Who do you think is going to tell her your needs in lovemaking if you don't?

9. **Love your wife as a person.** Husbands win the affection of their wives by loving them as a person, showering their attention and affection on them. I hope your wife never feels she must say, "The only time my husband is interested in me is when he wants sex." That is a

sad commentary on a husband's relationship with his wife.

FOR WIVES:

1. **Maintain a positive mental attitude** about lovemaking, about yourself, and about your husband. The wife's attitude toward all three of these areas will determine success or failure. Love is a vital emotion that grows or dies in direct proportion to one's thinking pattern. If you gripe and criticize your partner in your mind, before long love will die. But if you replace that negative pattern with praise and thanksgiving for the good qualities in your spouse, love will blossom.

2. **Relax! Relax! Relax!** I understand at first there will be nervous excitement, but after many repeated times relaxation should come. A wife's relaxation is important to her lovemaking because it helps prepare her.

3. **Chunk your inhibitions.** Though modesty is an admirable virtue for a Christian woman, it is out of place in the bedroom with her husband. A fine Christian woman admitted that she felt guilty when she let her husband watch her disrobe. She said, "My mother taught me that good women never do that kind of thing." She was counseled that what her mother told her was a mistake. But even after she tried to overcome this guilt, she had problems. Gradually she learned to enjoy the excitement she felt in that situation and her marriage was saved as a result.

4. **Remember that men are stimulated by sight.** Many women counselors urge women to make the daily homecoming of their husband the most significant time of the day. By bathing and fixing herself up she can give her husband an enthusiastic welcome home. Some women resent this type of thinking, but others practice it and reap the benefits.

5. **Never nag, criticize, or ridicule.** Nothing turns a man off faster than motherly nagging, or criticism, or ridicule of his manhood.

A brilliant doctor with a beautiful, cultured wife had an affair with a woman who had almost no education and was not nearly so attractive as his wife. Why did he do it? He said, "She makes me feel comfortable." The wife on reflection realized she had become very critical of his actions and work habits. He had sought a haven of peace somewhere else. Of course, I don't approve of his action, it was a sin. But often people are motivated to do the wrong things for the wrong reasons.

6. **Remember that you are a responder.** Most women admit to having exciting experiences they would never otherwise have attempted except in response to something initiated by their husbands.

The nature of the wife's response to the husband's advances often

75

determines the outcome of the sexual relation. If her response is indifferent, the husband will stop right there. But if she will cuddle close to him for a few minutes and accept his advances, she will gradually find her mood beginning to match his.

7. **Observe daily feminine hygiene.** This is important for two reasons: (1. Some women emit vaginal fluids, that have a strong odor. Unless you bathe regularly, it produces a very offensive odor. (2. Many women become immune to their own body odor. In this day and age of all kinds of soaps and lotions, odors should never be a problem.

8. **Communicate freely.** One big misconception is that the husband knows all about sex. Men are definitely interested, but few have ever taken the time to go to proper sources of information. The wife must learn to communicate freely about her sexual needs. Besides telling him how she feels, she should guide his hands to show him what gives her pleasure. Unless she tells him what excites her, he may never know.

9. **When all else fails, pray.** I believe by prayer God will help a couple have a successful sexual relationship. He has placed within each of us the sexual capabilities which He meant for us to enjoy. The only real prohibition relates to their use outside of marriage.

Carl Brecheen has given ten suggestions for husbands and wives that have to do specifically with enhancing the sexual part of their marriage.[4]

FOR HUSBANDS:

1. Tell her you love her every day and mean it.
2. Never pass up an opportunity to give her sincere praise.
3. Always speak to others of her in a complimentary way.
4. Communicate, but don't criticize.
5. Keep the spirit of courtship and romance alive in your marriage.
6. Take plenty of time for sex.
7. Discover the areas of her body which are particularly pleasurable to her.
8. Be careful of your cleanliness and personal hygiene.
9. Remember that your wife cannot respond as she would like when her feelings are hurt, when the setting is inappropriate, or when the children are stirring in the next room.
10. Communicate to her what she means to you.

FOR WIVES:

1. Keep personal attractiveness at its very best.
2. Be careful to be clean and to take care of personal hygiene.

3. Take extended time for lovemaking away from distractions.
4. Read some good books.
5. Let go of all inhibitions and participate fully and eagerly.
6. Welcome his advances.
7. Become actively involved in the process leading up to the sexual encounter.
8. Let him know what pleases you.
9. Be creative in initiating lovemaking.
10. Reassure him of his manliness.

The **Song of Solomon** is an Old Testament book that is full of special assignments that couples can do to vitalize a sexual relationship that has become boring repetition and lacking in romance.[5]

1. **Encourage the couple to go on a weekly date.** In chapter 7:11; 8:14, Solomon and Shulamith resolved their time pressure problems by deciding to go on a trip over night. In the countryside as they spent the night together, they would give their love to each other.

2. Another suggestion for couples who complain for always being too tired for sex is to **schedule times for sex.** Solomon and Shulamith spent time together to strengthen their bond. (2:8-17). Couples need to take the pressures off and allow their partners time to relax and change gears. This time should be spent in closeness, touching, and enjoying positive communication with each other.

One Houston Gynecologist recommended to not have sex after 7:00 p.m. Some would say, "Well, when should you have it?" I don't totally agree with that statement, but it does say something about timing.

3. **See sex as an opportunity to have fun and to "recharge."** Solomon praised his wife in a very joyful and cheerful manner. (6:4-10).

4. **Couples who fall into a monotonous rut need to be encouraged to be creative.** Solomon used a variety of methods to create romance in his relationship. He used poetry, 4:1-7; they walked together, 7:11-13; he used variety in their loveplay, 7:1-11; he created a great atmosphere for lovemaking, 1:16-17.

5. Husbands and wives need to be **taught that sexual desires for the body of one's mate is right and good.** Shulamith thought about her husband during the day, "My beloved is white and ruddy, chief among ten thousand." 5:10-15.

Wives need to be aggressive and totally available. Husbands must be sensitive and talk, talk, talk. Any waning of sexual desire that is not satisfactory to the other partner should be talked about together, and prayed about. Otherwise, resentments and bad feelings will result.

6. **Sexual problems should be solved quickly by repentance.** 5:2-8.

Husbands and wives have to take responsibility for their own actions and not blame their mate.

Dr. Ed Wheat gives the B.E.S.T. formula[6] for married couples to build their relationship. "B" for blessings not cursing, "E" for edifying, "S" for sharing, and "T" for touching (non-sexual). Practice his formula. It works! Once couples have grown to have a strong bond in their sexual relationship, they must also know that because of that bond, they can grow closer to God. When God is a part of their relationship, it is at its height.

Questions On Chapter 9

1. Are Christian couples supposed to enjoy the sexual relationship in marriage?

2. What scripture best supports the belief that sex in marriage is holy?

3. What suggestion given by Tim LaHaye for the husband is most needed in your marriage?

4. What suggestion given by Tim LaHaye for the wife is most needed in your marriage?

5. What one thing would you like to say to your partner to help improve your sexual relation?

[1]Ed Wheat, "Sex Problems And Technique In Marriage," Springdale, Arkansas: Bible Believers Cassettes.

[2]Robert Levin and Amy Levin, "Sexual Pleasure: The Surprising Preferences in 100,000 Women," **Redbook,** September, 1975, p. 53.

[3]Tim and Beverly LaHaye, **The Act Of Marriage,** Grand Rapids, Michigan: Zondervan Publishing House, 1976. Used by permission.

[4]Carl Brecheen and Paul Faulkner, **What Every Family Needs,** Austin, Texas: Sweet Publishing Company.

[5]"Counseling Married Couples With Sexual Problems," **Quarterly Newsletter for Christian Family Services, Gainsville, Florida,** October, 1987.

[6]Ed Wheat, **Love Life For Every Married Couple,** Springdale, Arkansas: Bible Believers Publishers. Used by permission.

Sex Questionnaire

1. Do you believe sex in marriage is:

    (a) Good
    (b) Evil

2. Do you believe an extra marital sexual experience:

    (a) Enhances a marriage
    (b) Is wrong

3. Our frequency of sex is about right.

    (a) Yes
    (b) No

4. I would describe our sexual relationship as:

    (a) Monotonous
    (b) Exhilarating, fulfilling, and romantic
    (c) Often one of us rejects the other's advances

5. My mate and I talk openly and honestly about sex; especially what we like and don't like.

    (a) Yes
    (b) No

6. Who initiates sex?
    (a) Husband
    (b) Wife
    (c) Both at different times

7. Sex should be used as reward or punishment.

    (a) Yes
    (b) No

8. Staying attractive to each other is important.

    (a) Yes
    (b) No

9. Our sexual relationship is characterized by:

    (a) Sensitivity, warmth, foreplay, and understanding
    (b) None of the above

10. If we were having sexual problems in our marriage we would:

    (a) Work them out ourselves
    (b) Say it is hopeless and give up
    (c) Seek counsel from a skilled Christian counselor

PART II: Family Relations
CHAPTER 10

The Family As God Wants It

T here are many good families and they are growing. I like what the father said about his growing family, "We no sooner sold the baby bed, than. . ." The future of the Christian home looks brighter than it has in a long time, but we will have to work at maintaining the Bible concept of the family.

It seems that the family is under a state of siege. There are all kinds of pressures on the family today. TV, modern philosophies, the homosexual community are all trying to change our understanding of the home. But the family, as the Bible teaches, is still the basic unit of society which undergirds all else. It is a universal phenomenon, because in every nation in the world, we find the family unit in various degrees. It is designed to fulfill all kinds of purposes, but one of the major purposes is to *prepare children for life*. Therefore, BALANCE in the family is needed.

There are different forms for the family today in our society. Before you close your mind, let me explain. We normally think of a family as father, mother, and children. This is the basic family unit, and the Bible concept of a complete family. But there are many families today that do not fulfill that design for the family. But many of these various forms are SUCCESSFUL in doing what a family is supposed to do.

Some know of my family background. I was raised in one of those different forms, the single parent family. My father died when I was three years of age and my mother chose not to marry again. There are a significant number of families like that in the United States and the numbers are growing. Not all are widowed, many are divorced, which is a group that has its own special set of problems for the parents and the children. This form of the family can accomplish the purpose of the family, it is harder, but it can be done.

I like to call the divorced family a "blended family" because in many cases you have 'yours, mine, and our" children. This family unit has special needs that must be met if it is to succeed.

I believe the "widowed" family has a better chance to succeed because the children still have just one set of parents. The deceased parent is still loved and held in esteem by the family, he or she is just gone. While in the "divorced" family, hatred, anger, ill feelings characterize the parents' relationship. The children often are confused about which parent is right, or which one to follow, or sometimes blame themselves for the whole problem.

The thing that makes any of these various forms of the family succeed is when the family accomplishes what God designed it to do - that is give the child a balanced, stable environment in which to learn and grow to Christian maturity.

Therefore, even families that have both parents - a mother and father - can fail when the parents don't follow God's directives for the family.

Let me give you some PICTURES of the family as I see God envisioning the family.

1. **The family is a place to grow people.** It is to be a balanced environment to grow human beings.

I believe NATURE teaches us this lesson about growing things. I like to watch the "National Geographic" specials on TV. Often they talk about survival in the land, or of a specific animal. Nature has a balance, each plant and each animal has a place in the balance of things. When the balance is upset, disastrous things can happen.

I believe the present famine in Ethiopia and Northern Africa is an example. Man interfered with the migration of the tribes and their herds, as a result, famine occurred.

So it is with man. Scripture says of Jesus, "(He) increased in wisdom, and stature, and in favor with God and men." Luke 2:52. This is a description of the balance in growth of our Savior and we should imitate His life. Jesus developed His body and His mind. He developed socially and He grew spiritually. This is the kind of balanced growth and development each of us wants for our children. But to achieve it we need a good father influence and a good mother influence in these areas to give the child a balanced environment.

Judy and I counsel with many families. The thing that we see over and over in these families is a break down in balance. Maybe a father no longer has time to function in his role as a leader, trainer, teacher, lover and provider. He spends all his time providing for the family that he forgets about the other areas, as a result, the children rebel, the wife rebels.

Maybe a mother stops performing in her role as a lover, emotion provider, and counselor. As a result the balance is gone. The children's growth and maturity in a proper fashion are upset.

How do you solve it? RESTORE THE BALANCE! Sometimes tough decisions have to be made about careers, or where to live, but if the needs of the family are considered the right choices can be made.

The following traits have been given for a HEALTHY family:

- Affirms and supports one another.
- Teaches respect for others.
- Develops a sense of trust.
- Teaches right and wrong.
- Exhibits a sense of shared responsibility.
- Has a strong sense of family.

2. The family is the most important center for the development of creativity.

- The family is where SELF-TRUST and SELF-ESTEEM are developed, which is at the heart of all creativity.
- The family is where SELF-DISCIPLINE is deveoped, which frees a person to be creative.
- The family provides the fertile soil in which individuals gifts, talents, and interests can be encouraged to develop and mature.

We need to see the family as the main center for creativity.

Not long ago I met a man who was a professional musician. It was interesting to me how that every member of his family, wife and children, had learned to play some musical instrument by his help and encouragement. They had formed a band and made beautiful music together, for their own enjoyment, as a family.

Around our house, sometimes the girls run upon a problem in school or in their personal relationships. They usually moan, "I can't do it!" Mom and Dad will say, "Why sure you can! Don't you remember Philippians 4:13, 'I can do all things through Christ who strengthens me.'" The girls usually laugh and say, "Oh yes, I forgot," or "O Dad!" That thought has developed in them the self-value they need to accomplish in this life.

The family is the center for developing self-trust and self-value. I really get excited when I see a father taking time, on a daily basis, to encourage and play and train his children. The father on the tennis court with his son, or on the golf course, or baseball field, or hunting, or doing homework, or mother helping her child make cookies, or sew, or do some other work. The family is the center for developing creativity!

3. **The family is the shelter from the storms of life.** A place where the whole family can feel safe and secure.

Recently in *Psychology Today,* a survey was conducted to rank 18 values in order of importance to the family. The number one choice, by a wide margin, was FAMILY SECURITY. Some of the other top values were self-respect, happiness, and true friendship.

Life does have it storms for each of us, and the family not only provides a place of shelter, but it can actually draw us closer together, as it provides that security we need.

Let me remind the adults that sometimes we forget how traumatic even the smallest event can be for a child. Things we pass off as unimportant can be devastating to a child.

A child falls and skins his knee, he needs a place to run to, and a person to run to who will comfort him and make him feel safe. The child learns early in life that the family is that kind of place, a sanctuary to which he can go when the storms come.

The storm may be a lost pet. At our home in Fort Smith, Arkansas, we had more cats than most people have in a life time. Everytime we would get a new one, Judy and I would run over it with the car. We all would cry over the loss, my youngest especially. She needed someone to put their arms around her and comfort her as she grieved the loss of her cat. It was important!

Sometimes we feel teenagers don't need this shelter, but they do! They come home and go into their room, shut the door, and get lost in their own world of music, or the TV, or study, or the phone. They are becoming more and more independent, at least they want you to feel that way. But they still need the support of familiar people, objects, and routine. They need times when parents talk to them about problems and give them guidance about a decision that has to be made. They still need loving arms that reach out to them and give support and encouragement.

Adults need family support and desire family support. I know as a father I want to feel that my family is supportive of decisions I have to make that affect their future also. When illness, or reversals, or disappointments occur, we have a place and a group of people who love us and accept us no matter what. That is FAMILY! We feel secure there.

One man I counseled with who had lost his job said, "If it weren't for the support of my family I think this experience would sink me."

There is nothing stronger than the love, concern and support of a family for each of its members.

4. One other picture of the family I want to draw is **the family as the transmitter of values from one generation to the next.**

The apostle Paul writing to Timothy about his faith gives us a beautiful illustration of this:

> *"I do call to remembrance the genuine faith that is in you, which dwelt first in your grandmother Lois and your mother Eunice, and I am persuaded is in you also."* 2 Timothy 1:5.

Paul was describing the great faith he saw in his young co-worker, Timothy. It was a faith that had been vital generation after generation. It was not like passing along a family heirloom, but something that had to be internalized with love and communication, and developed in this young man.

One of the values we need to transmit to our children is that *people are more important than things.* The best place to learn how to treat people is in the home, where opportunities abound to show love and respect. In day to day situations the child can learn how to show respect for life, others and himself.

In Paul's description of family roles and relationships, (Ephesians 5:21 - 6:4) the key to all of the relationships is a SELF-GIVING LOVE. Love is not just a feeling, but an action. Love is wanting what is best for the other person so much you don't worry about the cost to yourself.

I believe when children learn this, then real growth can occur. This value is one of the greatest values a child can learn, but he learns it as our generation transmits it to his generation.

Let me close with a survey by Delores Curran, author of **Traits of a Healthy Family.**[1] She asked 500 professionals in five related family fields to select from a list of 56 traits, the most common traits they find in a healthy family. She was surprised to receive 110% response to her questionnaire. Apparently some of those asked to participate made copies of the survey and gave it to their colleagues.

Below are the 56 traits listed, make your own choices about the 15 most important for a healthy family.

_____ 1. Communicates and listens.

_____ 2. Is affirming and supportive of one another.

_____ 3. Has a balance of interaction among members.

_____ 4. Develops trust.

_____ 5. Has a sense of play and humor.

_____ 6. Respects the privacy of one another.

_____ 7. Fosters family tabletime and conversation.

_____ 8. Fosters individual dining habits.

_____ 9. Exhibits a sense of shared responsibility.

_____10. Shares leisure time together.

_____11. Encourages individual use of leisure time.

_____12. Has strong sense of family; treasures family traditions.

_____13. Honors its elders.

_____14. Looks forward to the adolescent years.

_____15. Able to let go of grown children.

_____16. Prays together.

_____17. Has a shared religious core.

_____18. Permits religious flexibility among members.

_____19. Is not religion oriented.

_____20. Admits to and seeks help with problems.

_____21. Feels problems are private responsibility of family.

_____22. Allows members to be part of their peer culture.

_____23. Shares the same values.

_____24. Accepts and encourages individual values.

_____25. Values the work ethic.

_____26. Values college.

_____27. Values high income.

_____28. Values work satisfaction.

_____29. Values service to others.

_____30. Is consumer-oriented; finds gratification in goods.

_____31. Is cause- or movement-oriented.

_____32. Values rural or small-town mores.

_____33. Values metropolitan mores.

_____34. Values risk and courage, public acting out of principles.

_____35. Values going along and keeping peace.

_____36. Teaches a sense of right and wrong.

_____37. Teaches respect for others.

_____38. Operates from a base of parental rules.

_____39. Operates from a base of mutually negotiated rules.

_____40. Operates from a base of few or no rules.

_____41. Establishes roots in one community.

_____42. Is mobile, living in many communities.

_____43. Is known and respected in the neighborhood.

_____44. Treasures privacy over community affairs.

_____45. Is active in community affairs.

_____46. Is heavily involved in "little league" type activities.

_____47. Volunteers freely for school/church type activities.

_____48. Has control of family time and calendar.

_____49. Is a heavily-viewing television family.

_____50. Is a moderately-viewing television family.

_____51. Views relatively little television.

_____52. Is financially secure.

_____53. Has two parents living at home.

_____54. Has a wife/mother who does not work outside the home.

_____55. Has three or fewer children.

_____56. Owns its own home.

Below are the 15 traits given by the professionals. Compare your list with theirs:

1. Communicates and listens.
2. Affirms and supports one another.
3. Teaches respect for others.
4. Develops a sense of trust.
5. Has a sense of play and humor.
6. Exhibits a sense of shared responsibility.
7. Teaches a sense of right and wrong.
8. Has a strong sense of family in which rituals and traditions abound.
9. Has a shared religious core.
10. Has a balance of interaction among members.
11. Respects the privacy of one another.
12. Values service to others.
13. Fosters family table times and conversation.
14. Shares leisure time.
15. Admits to and seeks help with problems.

   1. Communicates and listens.[2] No one person should dominate the conversation of the family. Husbands and wives are genuine partners. One specialist said,

> "The healthiest families I know are ones in which the mother and father have a strong, loving relationship between themselves. This strong primary relationship seems to breed security in the children."

Another specialist said,

> "Where there is real communication the family has control over the TV. TV is a marvelous instrument, but not if it stifles

all conversation."

Dr. Lee Salk, Cornell University child psychologist said,

"Mealtime is incredibly important. . .people used to talk and listen at mealtime, but now we sit in front of the TV - take that time to be with your children."

2. **They affirm and support one another.** Dr. David Mace, a marriage specialist, did a study of families in Oklahoma.

"The purpose of this study was to find out if possible the source of strength in these families. Was there something they all had in common that made them function so effectively?"

Yes, there was, the study found that the members of these families liked each other and kept on telling each other that they liked each other. The result was that they enjoyed being together.

3. **Respect for others.** This is not easy. As we watch our children grow up, it is not easy to allow them to develop their own personality. It is difficult in the adolescent years to give them the privacy they need. We are tempted to make all their decisions for them - career, leisure, time, goals. Individuality has to be respected.

4. **Basic trust.** Dr. Jerry M. Lewis, director of the Timberlawn Psychiatric Center in Dallas, did a study on healthy families. In his survey of these families he found many differences, but he did not find one case of *infidelity*. It just did not occur in happy families. In his interviews with the couples he found that this infidelity was not due to lack of opportunity, but to a felt need to preserve trust in each relationship.

In healthy families trust extends to the relationship between parents and children. Parents do what they say, if a father says he will come to the school play, he comes. This builds trust between the father and his child. Also, it helps the child learn how to be trustworthy.

5. **They have time for play and humor.** The family doesn't wait for free time, they schedule it into the calendar. The family that pays attention to its need for play - a picnic, ball game, museum trip - usually has a healthier relationship.

Humor is very important also. A family hangs on to a story that they can recall with laughter. Mealtime becomes a place of joy and laughter as they recall amusing episodes of past days. Unhappy families may laugh at each other, but happy families laugh with each other.

6. **The importance of little rituals.** Flowers sent at birthdays, anniversaries remembered, simple gifts sent when they are unex-

pected, notes that express love and appreciation for the wife and children, all have a great power.

Also, rituals in the happy families may involve special moments when only two of the family members are present. Mom and dad need time by themselves, but so do mother and daughter, and father and daughter. These special times when they shop, or play a sport, or go to a ball game will provide valuable cement for their relationship.

7. **Shared religious core.** The movie *Fiddler On The Roof* is a powerful example of the strength of a family's religious custom. The family that has a rich legacy of faith and real ties that bind will pass along a sense of identity, of belongingness, of comfort and security to the next generation.

There are many other traits that could be emphasized. Happy families keep criticism within limits, they know how to forgive, and "bury the hatchet." Most of all, they know all the little gestures of affection are necessary to keep the family healthy. Most important they have learned how to say, "I am sorry, will you forgive me," and do it.

Alan Loy McGinnis in her book, *The Friendship Factor,* said that one of the basic rules for maintaining friendship is to "Assign top priority to your relationship." The same is true for the family. We have got to reaffirm the family. We have got to hang on the walls of our heart and mind all the pictures of what a good, happy, healthy family is like. Then we can have one!

Questions

1. What is your family background? How much do you feel this background has influenced your family life?

2. Do you feel your children have a good family in which to grow up? What would you have done differently in raising your children?

3. Of the pictures for the family listed in this chapter, which one is important to you? Why?

4. What talents as a young person do you feel you were never allowed to develop? Do those feelings cause you to assist your children in developing their talents?

---

[1]Delores Curran, **Traits of a Healthy Family,** Minneapolis, Minn: Winston Press, 1983.

[2]Harold Hazelip, "Traits of a Happy Family," **UpReach,** January, 1985, published by Highland Church of Christ, Abilene, Texas.

CHAPTER 11

The Christian Mother

The word "Mother" is the softest word in our language. There is no single definition that would perfectly describe what a mother is and what she does. It would take volumes of words put together by people who have had loving mothers and then there would be some qualities left out. I can only say it is a God given blessing bestowed upon women for their own well-being and for the well-being of the child.

God has given to womankind the unique and exclusive privilege of cooperating with Him to give life to another human soul. This act is as close to creation as we human beings can possibly come. Man has never yet and never will be able to create life as God does. Oh, he may be able to raise a test tube baby, or take the DNA from one cell and use it to make another. But, man will never be able to create that life-giving force in the cell itself because that right belongs to God. He has granted to womankind the privilege of cooperating with Him in this privilege of creation.

God gave the command in Genesis 1:28, "Be fruitful and multiply; fill the earth and subdue it." Everyone has a mother. But it seems that some women are rebelling against this honor and privilege. The women of the Old Testament considered having a child a great honor. *Sarah* pleaded with God to have a child. She was overjoyed when she found out that God had opened her womb so she could be a mother. *Hannah* also pleaded with God for a son and when it happened she praised God for blessing her and dedicated her son to the work of God.

Some women today feel it is an imposition to have children. They might lose their figure, or have to stop working, or have to give up something they feel more important. Consider Paul's instruction to young women:

"I desire that the younger widows marry, bear children, manage the house, give no opportunity to the adversary to speak reproachfully." 1 Timothy 5:14.

He says in Titus 2:4,5:

"Admonish the young women to love their husbands, to love their children, to be discreet, chaste, homemakers, good, obedient to their own husbands, that the word of God may not be blasphemed."

Many women don't know which way to turn, to go after a career or to marry or what! I believe the greatest work a woman can do is to marry and have children. It is the highest calling for womankind today. Now, don't misunderstand what I am saying, I am not saying a woman can't pursue a career or work at a job outside the home. I am saying that scripture says the greatest work anyone can do is mold the life of another person into someone who contributes to our world. I agree. That is the essence of motherhood.

Our society is peculiar in the way it measures prestige or importance. In Washington D.C. there stands a 12 foot statue of a man who was one of the greatest leaders of our land, Abraham Lincoln. A master craftsman carved the statue out of a solid block of white marble. As you stand before it and look at his face you can almost feel his soul, his character, and his compassionate heart. Who did the greatest favor for mankind, the man that carved the statue, or the mother who produced the man? Very few people visit the grave of Mary Hanks Lincoln. No plays or novels have been written about her. She is forgotten, but even the man himself, Lincoln said, "All that I am and can ever hope to be, I owe to my angel mother."

I don't want to leave the impression that being a baby factory is all that a woman should be. God expects more than just having a child, he wants her to help in the spiritual growth and well-being of the child.

One Christmas Day a little boy, who for the first two years of his life was normal in every way, was beaten by his mother. His parents had been out celebrating Christmas by getting drunk. They had left the little boy in a filthy house sleeping on a pile of rags. The fire was going and the room stayed warm until mom and dad got home. They fell into bed in a drunken stupor. They closed the fire place and the room got cold so the little boy attempted to climb into bed with them to get warm. She slapped him out into the floor and when he tried to come back she held him up and beat him about the face and neck with the buckle end of a belt. His skull was shattered in many places, and he had to be operated on repeatedly. A seven inch scar was on one side of his face and he was partially paralyzed. This woman brought this little

91

boy into the world, but she wasn't my idea of what it takes to be a real mother.

Emerson said, "Men are what their mothers make them."

Napoleon said, "The destiny of the child is always the work of the mother."

Statesmen, preachers, elders, lawyers, doctors, are all the products of their mother's knee. But the sad reality is that all liars, drunkards, cheats, gamblers, killers are also made on their mother's knee.

Remember Paul's words about Timothy, "I call to remembrance the genuine faith that is in you, which first dwelt in your grandmother Lois and your mother Eunice, and I am persuaded is in you also." 2 Timothy 1:5. A child that has a Christian mother is fortunate indeed.

I feel the importance of a good Christian mother can't be exaggerated. At the heart of every good thing is a tiny seed planted by some mother. Her deeds and words have done more to inspire men than any other work in the world.

The following **Parable for Mothers** expresses her work very beautifully:

> The young mother set her foot on the path of life. "Is the way long?" she asked.
>
> And her guide said, "Yes, and the way is hard. And you will be old before you reach the end of it. But the end will be better than the beginning."
>
> But the young mother was happy, and she would not believe that anything could be better than these years. So she played with her children, and gathered flowers for them along the way, and bathed with them in the clear streams; and the sun shone on them, and life was good, and the young mother cried, "Nothing will ever be lovelier than this."
>
> Then night came, and a storm, and the path was dark, and the children shook with fear and cold, and the mother drew them close and covered them with her mantle, and the children said, "Oh, Mother, we are not afraid, for you are near and no harm can come." And the mother said, "This is better than the brightness of day, for I have taught my children courage."
>
> And the morning came, and there was a hill ahead, and the children climbed and grew weary, and the mother was weary, but at all times she said to the children, "A little patience, and we are there." So the children climbed, and when they reached the top, they said, "We could not have done it without you, Mother." And the mother, when she lay down that night, looked up at the stars, and said, "This is a better

day than the last, for my children have learned fortitude in the face of hardness. Yesterday, I gave them courage; today I have given them strength."

And the next day, strange clouds came which darkened the earth - clouds of war and hate and evil, and the children groped and stumbled, and the Mother said, "Look up. Lift your eyes to the Light." And the children looked, and saw above the clouds an Everlasting Glory, and it guided them and brought them beyond the darkness. And that night the mother said, "This is the best day of all, for I have shown my children God."

And the days went on, and the weeks and the months, and the years, and the mother grew old, and she was little and bent. But her children were tall and strong, and walked with courage, and when the way was rough they lifted her, for she was as light as a feather; and at last they came to a hill, and beyond the hill they could see a shining hill and golden gates flung wide.

. . .Selected. . .

The old maxim is still true: "The hand that rocks the cradle, rules the world."

I do feel there are some fallacies in our thinking about what it takes to be a good parent. In the thinking of some when a young girl is old enough to have a child she is old enough to be a mother. That is not true! It is only with God's help and daily communion with God that a woman can expect to meet the challenge of being a mother. Most teens are not mature enough to meet this type of commitment.

The motto of motherhood should be,

> *"Be anxious for nothing, but in everything by prayer and supplication, with thanksgiving, let your requests be made known to God; and the peace of God, which surpasses all understanding, will guard your hearts and minds through Christ Jesus."* Philippians 4:6,7.

A mother doesn't need to waste her time worrying about useless things, because that time and energy needs to be spent on her family.

Consider these steps of good Christian mothering:

1. The primary step is **she must be a Christian.** If she has not made a commitment to Christ herself, she will be a weak foundation to build the lives of her children. (Acts 2:38, 8:26-40).

Mothers need to set the example of a great faith in God. If she has a little faith her children will be people of little faith. She is the key in building their faith.

Also, mothers need to let their children see that God is important to them by the example of faith they set in day to day living.

2. The mother is to **set a proper attitude toward God and the church.** The mother is responsible for the spiritual attitude of the whole family. I don't mean to minimize the importance of the father in training his children, but the mother can make sure that time is spent for home worship and Bible study. She can set the tone for worship at home and even at the church building. If everyone is rushed, or there is fighting at home before you go to worship, it is very hard to have a spirit of adoration to God.

God has promised us, "Train up a child in the way he should go, And when he is old he will not depart from it." Proverbs 22:6. *Training* is not just your influence, but it is directing, and teaching, and loving a child in the direction of God.

3. A good mother must be **concerned about the physical well-being of her children.** The gospel writer, Luke, said of Jesus, "He increased in wisdom and stature, and in favor with God and men." Luke 2:52. That means he grew physically, intellectually, and socially. We must be concerned about the growth of our children in all these same areas.

Mothers need to teach their children the proper care of their bodies. This includes: diet, personal cleanliness, exercise, and dangers facing the physical body. Also, I believe she must teach them about modesty and other Christian standards for personal health. Remember, "Your body is the temple of the Holy Spirit." 1 Corinthians 6:19.

4. Mothers need to **encourage their children to grow intellectually.** She should encourage them to read good books, see good movies, listen to good music, etc. Do the things that will help that child grow in wisdom.

5. Mothers should **provide for positive recreation for their children.** Christians have to say NO about so many things the world considers fun and entertainment. We need to provide entertainments that our children can do without fear of losing their Christian standards. We MUST provide alternatives. I want my home open to my children and their friends. I want it to be a place they can go and have fun. It is a place that other kids talk about. Not in a bad light, but wishing their home and parents were like that.

6. The mother must **teach her children to be responsible.** I feel this is one of the greatest shortcomings of our day. We give our children too much without letting them earn it or ever be responsible for it. Parents say, "I want them to be independent," but what we create is a nation full of dependent children. They have never earned money themselves and learned the value of the struggle.

We do chores ourselves that we should let our children do, so we can hurry and get finished. They can't learn responsibility until we give it to them.

I believe many of the heartbreaks of today can be traced back to a home where nothing was required of the children, everything was done for them. Youth want to feel they are doing something worthwhile and good. Let's give them the chance to do that. They will surprise you as to the quality of work they can do if you take the time to show them how to do it.

Included in this work is the church. Some parents don't want their children to be involved with the church activities because it will reflect on them that their children are doing more in the cause of Christ than they are. Let me encourage you to set an example for your children and encourge them to put GOD FIRST.

7. The final step is mothers must **discipline their children.** Discipline for failure to obey should be as prompt and certain as praise for achievement.

DISCIPLINE is from the same root word as DISCIPLE which means, a learner, a student. Discipline means to guide, or teach, or train a child in the right direction.

Most of the time we think of discipline as punishment. It can include punishment for wrong doing. But real discipline occurs before a child has to make a choice. His discipline helps him make the right choice. Let's love our children enough to discipline them.

On April 2, 1972, an unusual picket line occurred outside the Grinnell Company in Indianapolis. The family of Mrs. Glen Campbell was picketing the plant which had given her a full-time job five months before. The husband and four daughters were trying to get her fired so she could be at home with her family.

The five pickets carried signs which read, "I want mom;" "Mom or bust;" and "Mom, come home." Nearly 40% of all workers in this country are women and half of those women have children under the age of 18 years.

What this family was expressing to its mom was Mom we need you at home on a full-time basis. No baby-sitter can do what a mother can do with her own children.

You may call me a "male chauvinist", but I believe those children need that mom. And she needs to be there for them!

The late Judge Sam Tatum, Juvenile Court of Davidson County, Tennessee, made this statement:

> "I've had children tell me that they go into their homes and if mother isn't there the old house is just not the same. There is something missing. I would say to the working mother, unless

95

it is absolutely essential that you work to maintain the home, get out of that job, get back into the home with your children.

Now if you MUST work, God bless you and God give you strength. But if you're just working because you don't like the home, or you're just working for more money, then you're very likely trading the birthright of your children for a mess of pottage."

I believe Judge Tatum's message is not out of date, but it does hurt. I believe that not all working mothers have failed. I believe there is a time when the children are growing up and in school that work can be an important outlet for the mother. She may need to work outside the home. Each home is different and has its own personal needs, but the need of a mother is one of those needs that never changes.

Let me close with this personal illustration. On July 9, 1946 in the town of Tacoma, Washington, at Fort Lewis, there was born to a military family a baby boy that the parents named Eddie. Because the father was a military person, he was killed, about three years later, in an unfortunate set of circumstances. The mother was left to care for and raise five children on her own.

She did her best, not having a high school education, by baby-sitting and finally teaching kindergarten at one of the local churches. She always took care of her children and saw to their needs. She washed clothes, ironed them, cooked meals and worked all at the same time. Many a night was spent with the lamps burning til the early morning hours.

As I reflect over those years, I have a great deal to be thankful for because of my mother's attitude about life. She was one of those people who loved children. She was a friend to many of the children on our street. I remember many times young people coming to talk with her about the problems they were facing. She always gave them counsel or advice about what to do. She also gave me counsel about life and what I could achieve.

I also remember, on some cold and wintery Sunday mornings, when hardly any one else made it to Sunday School and church, we would always be there on time, wearing a tie and having our Bible lesson ready, I think! She loved God and relied on Him to see her and her family through the hard times.

I wish all men could have had a mother like mine. I really believe the world would be a better place. I realize she made mistakes. There were times when I rebelled against her counsel. But she loved her children and showed them her love and encouraged them to do the best they could. And they did!

Of her five children, four now have Master degrees from different universities. One son-in-law has his doctorate. Two of her sons are ministers. One is a military man. All are married and have children. All have a basic love for God and show their faith by their lives of service to God.

My mother doesn't have a great knowledge of the scripture, but because of her and the love of my wife, I am what I am today. I could have been anything I set my mind to, but because of their encouragement I am a lover of God and His ways.

I want to encourage the mothers that will read this book, don't cheat your family out of the one, most important thing you can do for them. BE A CHRISTIAN MOTHER!

Questions

1. What does the word "mother" mean to you? Give some personal examples of memories you have of your mother and the good influence she had on your life.

2. What qualities for a good Christian mother would you add to the list in this chapter? Discuss them.

3. In Proverbs 31:10-31, Solomon lists a number of qualities seen in the "worthy woman". List some of the ones you feel are important.

4. What qualities does your wife have that make her a good mother? Do you tell her she is a good mother?

CHAPTER 12

The Christian Father

One time there was a graduate student working on a project about juvenile delinquency. He was having a hard time collecting the data he wanted. His project involved phoning 12 homes about 9:00 p.m. to ask the parents if they knew where their teenagers were. He complained, "My first five calls were answered by teens who didn't know where their parents were."

The family, although it is the oldest human and divine institution, is not the most stable. Change is a central part of family life. Our children change daily before our eyes. The father is a key person in the family. He has to be an active participant in the changes that take place, or the destruction of the family can result.

David, the writer of Psalms, tells us in Chapter 127:3 that our children are a gift from God. David emphasizes to us that we need to be grateful to God for such a wonderous gift. There is no greater thrill than to see for the first time your own child. To look into its face and realize that this soul is from you and comes as a gift from God. It is a soul that has been entrusted to your care to mold and build into a person that believes in God and His Son. You literally hold the destiny of this beautiful child in the palm of your hand. But yet you turn around a few times and the child is grown up and gone away from home to make his mark in the world. Did you do all you could to prepare him for his future?

Erma Bombeck wrote an article in her syndicated column that really expresses what parents feel as they deal with children growing up and leaving home. She said:

> "One of these days you'll shout, 'Why don't you kids grow up and act your age?' And they will. Or, 'You guys get outside

and find yourself something to do and don't slam the door! And they won't. You'll straighten up the boys' bedroom neat and tidy, bumper stickers discarded, spread tucked and smooth, toys displayed on the shelves, hangers in the closet, animals caged, and you'll say out loud, 'Now I want it to stay this way.' And it will. You'll prepare a perfect dinner with a salad that hasn't been picked to death, and a cake with no finger traces in the icing, and you'll say, 'Now there's a meal for company.' And you will eat it alone. You'll say, 'I want complete privacy on the phone. No dancing around. No pantomimes. No demolition crews. Silence! Do you hear?' And you'll have it. There will be no more plastic tablecloths stained with spaghetti, no more bedspreads to protect the sofa from damp bottoms, no more gates to stumble over at the top of the basement stairs, no more clothes pins under the sofa, no more playpens to arrange a room around. You'll have no more anxious nights under a vaporizer tent, no more sand in the sheets, or Pop-eye movies in the bathroom, no more iron-on patches, wet, knotted shoestrings, tight boots, or rubber bands for pony-tails. Imagine, a lipstick with a point on it, and no baby-sitter for New Year's Eve. Washing only once a week, seeing a steak that isn't ground, having your teeth cleaned without a baby on your lap, no PTA meetings, no car pools, no blaring radios, no one washing her hair at 11 o'clock at night, having you own roll of Scotch tape. Think about it! There'll be no more Christmas presents out of toothpicks and library paste. No more sloppy oatmeal kisses, no more tooth fairy, no giggles in the dark, no knees to heal, no responsibility. Only a voice crying, 'Why don't you grow up?' And the silence echoing, 'I Did.' "

What causes a child to rebel against his father?[1]

1. When a father does not fulfill promises - he loses faith in his father.
2. When a father does not admit he is wrong - he loses confidence in his leadership.
3. When a father refuses to ask for forgiveness - he reacts to his father's pride.
4. When a father does not have the right priorities.
5. When a father is too strict in his discipline.
6. When a father neglects the word of God - he does also.
7. When a father delegates his child's Christian education to others.

Let me suggest four things that as a father I owe my children. I believe they are characteristics of what the Christian father should be.

1. A Christian father needs to **show his children he loves his wife.** In our chapter on love in marriage, I gave 1 Corinthians 13:4-7 as a definition of love. I believe unconditional love is described in that scripture. This is the type of love a father should demonstrate for his wife before his children. How can they know what marital love is all about unless they see it demonstrated in a positive fashion by mom and dad. I don't mean that the parents are to engage in intercourse in front of their children, but they need to see mom and dad kiss and hug, say endearing things to each other, touching each other in a loving fashion, and doing all the things that are expressions of love.

When Paul said, "Husbands, love your wives. . ." Ephesians 5:25, he told us how. Some men will say, "We all love our wives," but do we love them as Paul said? One thing he said, "as Christ also loved the church." He further said, "and gave Himself for it," Paul defines the amount of love a husband is to have for his wife. I would emphasize that the children need to see you, as father, "giving your life for her." Mom is important to every child. If that child sees dad treating mom in a rude fashion, or as a slave of the family, dad is put in a bad light, not mom. It is funny how children can so easily pick up on the fact that dad is treating mom bad, and dad can't even see it himself. Men wake up! Show your children how to love mom!

2. A Christian father **owes his children discipline for their lives.** Discipline is a mandate from God! "Train up a child in the way he should go, And when he is old he will not depart from it." Proverbs 22:6. "Fathers, do not provoke your children to wrath, but bring them up in the training and admonition of the Lord." Ephesians 6:4.

Unfortunately today, we think of discipline as punishment. But discipline is much more. It may include punishment when that is necessary, and it should be consistent and firm, but the real meaning of discipline is not a list of negative prohibitions, but the act of positive GUIDANCE and TRAINING. This is what Paul and Solomon both said.

Have you ever gone to a beautiful garden that showed evidence of loving, daily care? It takes DISCIPLINE to make a garden grow like that. You have to cut the grass, prune the plants, bend the branches, and shape the plants to make them grow on a trellis or follow a wire that is to hold the vines off the ground. Believe me, that takes time and understanding of the needs of each plant.

Young people are no different! They need limits set. They need time and guidance. They need teaching. Some parents are afraid to raise a child. They are afraid they might say the wrong thing or bend the child in the wrong direction. So they let the child go his own way, which is the worst thing they could do in terms of raising a child.

If you want to destroy a house you don't have to take an ax and break the windows out or chop up the floors and walls. Just let it alone and it will rot and decay and fall to pieces all by itself.

Our children are the same way. They are what we make of them. It is up to us to give them the guidance or discipline they need.

"He who spares his rod hates his son, But he who loves him disciplines him promptly." Proverbs 13:24.

One counselor of youth told of a girl who had come into his office several times. She was full of bitterness and antagonism, and her behavior was totally unacceptable at school, and at home. She gave the appearance of being a vicious and heartless person. As the counselor talked with her, she reached the point where she began to cry and blurted out, "I wish my daddy would come home and make me behave." She felt the need for limits she had not been able to place in her own life.

Some years ago the Houston, Texas Police Department published a list of *Rules for Raising Delinquent Children:*

First: Begin with infancy to give the child everything he wants. In this way he will grow up to believe that the world owes him a living.

Second: When he picks up bad words, laugh at him. This will make him thing he is cute. It will also encourage him to pick up "cuter" phrases that will blow off the top of your head later.

Third: Never give him any spiritual training. Let him wait until he is twenty-one and then "decide for himself."

Fourth: Avoid the use of the word "wrong." It may develop a guilt complex. This will condition him to believe later, when he is arrested for stealing a car, that society is against him and he is being persecuted.

Fifth: Pick up everything he leaves laying around - books, shoes, and clothing. Do everything for him so he will be experienced in throwing all responsibility on someone else.

Sixth: Let him read any printed matter he can get his hands on. Be sure to sterilize the silverware and drinking glasses, but let him feast on garbage.

Seventh: Quarrel frequently in the presence of your children. In this way they will not be too shocked when the home is broken up later. (I would add, that there are always disagreements in the home. When they occur let your children see you disagree, but also solve the problem, and fight fairly.)

Eighth: Give a child all the spending money he wants. Never let him earn his own. Why should he have things as tough as you had them?

Ninth: Satisfy his every craving for food, drink, and comfort. See that every sensual desire is gratified. Denial may lead to harmful frustrations. (Do you remember the comic strip character, teenaged Penny, who one day complained to her mother that her mother was going to frustrate her? Penny's mother said, "Dear, you have longer to get over your frustration than I have to get over mine!")

Tenth: Always take your child's part against neighbors, teachers, and policemen. They are all prejudiced against your children.

Eleventh: When he gets into real trouble, apologize for yourself by saying, "I never could do anything with that boy."

Twelfth: Prepare yourself for a life of grief. You are probably going to have it.

Obviously these are rules they don't want you to follow, but sadly some parents have unwittingly followed these rules to the letter.

3. A Christian father **owes his children LOVE.** Not only is he to show his love for his wife, but he is to show and give his love to his children.

Love is the basis of true discipline. Solomon and Paul, both said, "Whom the Lord loves He corrects." Proverbs 3:12, Hebrews 12:6. Why does God discipline us? Because He loves us! Let me emphasize that genuine love doesn't let a child have his way or let him get by with things that will destroy his character under the guise of love. Love is always concerned about proper conduct, proper respect, proper character, proper performance and the discipline that it takes to achieve it.

Love does include provision for the physical needs of life. "If anyone does not provide for his own, and especially for those of his household, he has denied the faith and is worse than an unbeliever." 1 Timothy 5:8.

Love is not overly protective or possessive. Sometimes the greatest demonstration of love comes when a parent knows when to turn loose.

102

Mother love is wonderful, but smother love is dangerous and can cause a child to rebel against its parents.

One of the greatest examples I ever saw of a parent turning loose was by a mother who brought a present to her son on his wedding day. It was beautifully wrapped and she asked him and his bride to unwrap it before the ceremony. Inside the box were two apron strings - untied. This was her way of saying, "I have turned loose - you two are on your own."

There was a lady who had a pet squirrel. The squirrel was a beautiful pet. It was so interesting to watch as he would take pecans, burst the hull from the nut and then eat the meat of the nut. One day the lady went shopping and bought a bag of shelled pecans. She said, "My little old squirrel won't have to burst the hulls anymore to get something to eat. Everything was fine, but in a few weeks, the squirrel got sick. She carried him to a veterinarian. He said, "My goodness, this squirrel's front teeth are growing too long. What's wrong, what are you feeding this squirrel?"

She answered, "Shelled pecans."

"You mean to tell me you're feeding this squirrel pecans that have already been hulled? Lady, don't you know that God made this creature to work for his food? That's part of nature for this squirrel to open up pecans with his teeth. You've got to stop putting shelled pecans in his cage."

The lady did as the vet said, but the squirrel turned up his nose at the pecans. He'd found another way to get food. Somebody was doing that work for him. He wasn't going to burst those old pecans and work for his food anymore. So the lady started giving him shelled pecans again, so he wouldn't die. But the squirrel's teeth had grown so long that now he could not chew his food and the little squirrel died. She had loved that squirrel so much it KILLED him. Don't do that to your children!

Also, love makes time. Time for companionship and togetherness. We live in a busy age, there are all kinds of demands on our time. But love demands that we make time for our children. Time is the most precious gift you can give your child.

4. Finally, a Christian father **owes spiritual training to his children.** Spiritual training is a key to proper growth for our children.

Deuteronomy 6:6-9 is a classic scripture on how to train your children.

> *"And these words which I command you today shall be in your heart; you shall teach them diligently to your children, and shall talk of them when you sit in your house, when you walk by the way, when you lie down, and when you rise up. You*

shall bind them as a sign on your hand, and they shall be as
frontlets between your eyes. You shall write them on the door-
posts of your house and on your gates."

Look at all the places and times you are to talk about God to your children. We are to use every method, every situation to teach our children God's word and ways.

This does include our example! Children are great imitators. They do what they see their parents doing. You may tell them to read their Bibles, but if they see you reading the newspaper or magazines all the time they know which is most important to you. They learn from your example what means the most to you.

The same is true about how much you really love God, the church, and the family. What you talk about and show an interest in is what you really love.

The sad thing is that we teach our children to lie, hate, cheat, and steal in the very same way. They come into the world pure and clean, sinless, then you and I teach them to hate others, lie about what we have done or were supposed to do, or to cheat in their dealings with others, to do all the evil things in our world. A parent will say about a bad habit, "I am not going to let my child do this when he grows up." But that child is already under the influence of that parent, and is imitating his every move. What chance does the child have to not do the bad habit? You have heard the old saying, "Like father, like son." It is still true!

I have counseled with many a parent whose teenage daughter has become pregnant. The mother will wonder how or why it happened, when she herself was unfaithful to her partner, or was constantly telling the daughter not to do it. Both of these statements were negative reinforcements of what she was trying to not get her daughter to do. With love and by her example she needed to teach the girl the moral standards needed to deal correctly with this temptation or situation.

Parents, it is a great responsibility to raise a child in Christ. We have to live a righteous life before them.

When you look your child in the face and wonder what he or she will be, understand, what he sees in YOU is what he will become.

If he sees love and respect for the Lord, concern for others, Christian character, devoted service, he will imitate these things in his own life.

Consider this story about the *Prodigal Father:*

A certain man had two sons and the younger said to him, "Father, give unto me that portion of thy time, thy attention, and the companionship and thy counselship which falleth unto me." And the father divided unto him his living, in that he paid the boy's bills, he sent him to a select preparatory school, to dancing school and to college and tried to make himself believe that he was doing his full duty by his son. And not many days hence, his father gathered together his interest, his aspirations, his ambitions, and he took a journey into a far country; into a land of stocks and bonds and securities and other such things which do not interest a boy. And there he wasted his precious opportunity of being a companion and a counsel and a guide for his son. And after he had spent the very best years of his life, he had money, but he had failed to find any real satisfaction; and there arose a mighty famine in his heart and he began to long for some genuine sympathy and friendship. And so he went down and joined himself to one of the clubs of that land. They elected him chairman of the house committee, president of the club and even sent him to congress but he fain would have satisfied himself with the husks that other men did not eat. No man gave unto him any real friendship, and when he had come to himself he said, "How many men of my acquaintance have sons whom they love and whom they understand. They seem perfectly at ease in the companionship of their sons, and I perish with heart hunger. I know what I will do. I will arise and I will go to my son and I will say unto him, "Son, I have sinned against thee and against Heaven, I am no longer worthy to be called thy father. Let me be as one of thy friends." And he arose and went to his son and while he was a long way off, his son saw him coming and he was moved with astonishment. And instead of running and falling on his neck the son drew back and was ill at ease and the father said unto him, "Son, I have sinned against Heaven and against thee, and I am no longer worthy to be called thy father, let me be as one of thy friends." And the boy said, "Not so, not so, I wish it were possible. There was a time when I longed for your companionship. There was a time when I asked for counselship, but you were always too busy. I got my companionship, but I got it in the wrong places. I got my advice, but I got the wrong kind and now alas I am a wreck in body and in soul, and it is too late, too late!"

I believe another part of our responsibility in spiritual training is providing a *Christian Education* where possible. I include in this not just formal education, as a Christian elementary, high school, and college, but church Bible classes and home Bible study.

Sometimes the formal Christian education is for only four years of college, but that type of training and guidance really needs to start before the college years. Many areas are very fortunate to have the opportunity to send their children to a Christian school from grade one. The number of Christian schools is growing.

But, some only give lip service to the value of Christian education. They say it is good and important, but never do anything to make it available to their children. Even on the college level this is true.

As a parent I have the responsibility to train my child, in the home, in the church, in every possible way, about the Lord. As a father, God will hold me responsible for what the family does to train its children.

Someone said, "Some things God gives often, some He gives only once. The seasons return again and again, the flowers change with the days. But, youth comes twice to no one."

Fathers, we have just ONE CHANCE with each of our children entrusted to our care by God. I pray that you will join me as I try my best to make that child's life one that is devoted to God. As I lead they will follow.

There is an old Chinese proverb that puts all this into perspective:

"If there is righteousness in the heart,
there will be beauty in the character.
If there is beauty in the character,
there will be harmony in the home.
If there is harmony in the home,
there will be order in the nation.
If there is order in the nation,
there will be peace in the world.

It all begins with righteousness in the heart. That comes from Christ as we live for Him.

Questions

1. In Psalm 127:3, David describes our children as gifts from God. Do you consider your children a gift from God? How do you show them they are a gift from God?

2. In the list of things that cause a child to rebel against its father, which one hurts you the most?

3. As a father what do you owe your children? Give a list of things you owe them and explain why you owe them.

4. How important is your example to your children? Do you really feel that you influence them by our attitudes and example?

5. Is "Love" a part of discipline?

¹Men's Manual, Institute In Basic Youth Conflicts, Inc., Oak Brook, Illinois.

CHAPTER 13

What Children Owe Their Parents

I t is important for us to recognize that family success does not rest exclusively in the fact that it is a divine institution. Nor, does the responsibility for proper conduct in the family rest exclusively with the parents. Young people in the family have a responsibility to make the family a success and provide proper conduct, also.

There has been a great deal of talk about a generation gap between teens and their parents. As a parent I see that gap, or at least some tension. But the responsibility to bridge this gap lies with both the parents and teenagers.

I think often teens fail to realize that many of the things required of them by their parents and other adults are expected because of the experiences that these adults have gone through.

I like to think of myself as a young man. I like to go to my hometown of Senatobia, Mississippi, because there I am still considered a young preacher. As the years go by that sounds more and more flattering, but my girls don't think of 'ole Dad that way. They see me as an older person. I am sure your children see you in the same light.

It is illustrated to us in the movie, **The West Side Story.** The boy who said to the older man who tried to help him, "But you were never my age!" YES, WE WERE YOUR AGE! Maybe not at the same time, nor have we experienced the exact same experiences, but we have been there nonetheless. Because man's needs and desires never change from one generation to another generation, there are certain expectations required of young people by their parents.

One teenager showing his frustration wrote, "The world is full of people who are quick to say, 'I was a boy once,' but who act as if they have never been."

Parents, we have a responsibility to our children to find a way to effectively communicate to them our love and understanding of their situation.

The complaint, "You just don't understand!" so often is true. Both sides have a responsibility to close that gap.

Let me address our young people about THEIR RESPONSIBILITY to the family.

1. One of the most difficult and yet most essential lessons for young people to learn is that some things are to be done simply because they are right.[1] I call this learning obedience!

"Children, obey your parents in the Lord, for THIS IS RIGHT." Ephesians 6:1. "Children, obey your parents in all things, for this is well pleasing to the Lord." Colossians 3:20.

Jesus gives us a good example of this obedient spirit. Luke tells us in chapter 2, verse 51, that Jesus went down to Nazareth and obeyed His parents in ALL things.

When Paul made his statements in Ephesians 6, he doesn't argue the point. He doesn't say, "Obey your parents because. . ." There are many reasons for the child to learn obedience, but the reason Paul gives here is simply, "for this is right." There are some things you do because they are RIGHT!

Rebellion against authority which always begins in the home, is an attitude that a person will carry with him all through life.

Recently I sat in a court room and heard the sordid details of how a 20 year old man took the life of an 18 year old man. The 20 year old had been arrested over 70 times for crimes and offenses in the last four years. He and his father would sit in their home and talk about all the people they wanted to kill, and how others treated them badly. The son finally turned his father's words into reality.

Parents often set a poor example for their children by having a bad attitude themselves toward authority.

For example, the father who always speaks critically about his boss at work, "He never does anything right," or "What he says makes no sense," or "The way he requires things to be done is stupid," is often rebellious against authority himself and is teaching his children to do the same thing.

This same parent is rebellious against authority at church. The elders are no good, the preacher is lousy, the song leader is off key.

He is rebellious against authority in the government. The police don't know what they are doing. The President and Congress at every level are crooked and irresponsible.

He files his Income Tax because he is afraid he would be caught if he didn't.

His spirit of rebellion is constantly exhibited before his children, and when they copy that spirit and rebel against him, he wonders what in the world has happened. Where did they learn that type of spirit.

Obedience at all ages is important! Some things are to be done simply because they are the right things to do.

2. When I read, "Children obey your parents. . ." I think of a small child obeying his mother. But, the next statement has no age limit on it, "Honor your father and mother." We never outgrow *our responsibility to be in subjection to our parents.*

Of course, there comes a time when we are no longer under the direct supervision of our parents, but the need to honor and care for them never ends, even when we move away from home.

I feel it is good for our children to get a perspective about who their parents are. *Bergan Evans,* a few years ago at Pennsylvania State University, gave the commencement speech to the graduating seniors. In his speech he introduced them to some very important people sitting next to them. It was their parents! He made these observations:

> "These are the people who in just five decades have increased life expectancy by approximately 50%, who while cutting the working day by a third have more than doubled the per capita output. These are the people who have given you a healthier world than they found, and because of this you no longer have to fear epidemics of flu, typhus, diphtheria, smallpox, scarlet fever, measles or mumps. And the dreadful polio is no longer a medical factor, while tuberculosis is almost unheard of. Let me remind you that these remarkable people lived through history's greatest depression. Many of these people know what it is to be poor and hungry and cold and because of this they determined that it would not happen to you, that you would have a better life. You would have food to eat, you would have milk to drink, vitamins to nourish you, a warm home, better schools, and greater opportunities to succeed. Because they gave you the best, you are the tallest, healthiest, brightest and probably the best looking generation ever to inhabit the land. Because they were materialistic, you will work fewer hours, learn more, have more leisure time, travel to more distant places, and have more of a chance to follow your life's ambition. These are also the people who fought man's grisliest war; they are the people who defeated the tyranny of Hitler, and who when it was all over had the

110

compassion to send billions of dollars to help their former enemies to rebuild their homelands. And these are the people who had the sense to begin the United Nations. It was representatives of these two generations who through the highest courts of the land fought racial discrimination, to begin a new era of civil rights. While they have done all these things, they've had some failures. They have not yet found an alternative for war, or for racial hatred. They have made more progress by the sweat of their brow than in any previous era, and don't you forget it. And if your generation can make as much progress in as many areas as these two generations have, you should be able to solve a good many of the earth's remaining ills. It is my hope and I know the hope of these two generations, that you find the answers to many of these problems that plague mankind, but it won't be easy. And you won't do it by negative thinking nor by tearing down or belittling. You can do it by hard work, humility, and faith in mandkind.''

I believe something like this should be written about every generation to call attention to their accomplishments. Their children need to see and understand what their parents have done.

3. One other lesson is Paul's teaching in Galatians 6:7, "Do not be deceived; God cannot be mocked. *A man reaps what he sows.*"

As a young person, don't think you can get by with lies and cheating in any form without reaping the disastrous results. Sin always brings a crop of disaster that has to be reaped.

I have heard some people advise youth to "Sow your wild oats while you are young." This is some of the worst advice anyone could give a younger person. Just because you are young doesn't mean you will not have to reap the harvest of your actions. Solomon, the wise man, said, "Remember now your Creator in the days of your youth." Ecclesiastes 12:1.

Religion is not something you do when you get so old you can't do anything else. It is for today! No matter your age, it is for you! Right now, as a youth, are some of the best years of your life for service and dedication to the cause of Christ. Please, don't prostitute yourself to sin.

You can get forgiveness from God for your sins. Even men who know forgiveness themselves will forgive you. But you can't erase the scars, you can't forget. The scars always remain.

The story is told of a little boy on the frontier of America. He was like most boys, always into trouble. So his father told him that every time he did something wrong he would nail a spike into the hitching post out front of their home. Well, it wasn't long until the post was full of spikes. It became a source of embarrassment to the little boy because everytime someone came to visit, they would always ask about the post and why all those spikes were in it and they would answer, "It's Johnny's sins."

So he asked his father how he could get the spikes out of the post. His father said, "Well, everytime you do a good deed I will take out one of the spikes." Johnny was pleased to hear that, so he started watching for good deeds to perform. He filled up the water bucket, filled up the wood pile, etc. The spikes started coming out until they were all out except one.

Well, everyone gathered around and cheered as the last spike came out, all except Johnny. He looked very sad and disappointed. His father asked, "What's the matter Johnny, you worked very hard to get all the spikes out and now that they are out you don't seem pleased."

Johnny looked at the post and said, "Yes, but the holes are still there!"

Johnny got rid of the wrongs (sins), but the evidence of the spikes, the holes, was still there. The hurt, the scars, always remain. There is nothing you can do to remove those scars. So, be very careful not to do something in your youth, or at any age, that will scar you for the rest of your life.

Someone has drawn up a list of six whimsical rules that help young people understand their parents better!

First: Don't be afraid to speak your parents' language. Try strange sounding phrases like, "I'll help with the dishes," and "Yes, I'll be glad to."

Second: Try to understand their music. Play Glenn Miller's "Moonlight Serenade" on the stereo until you are accustomed to the sound. (I would add some country music.)

Third: Be patient with the underachiever. When you catch your dieting mom sneaking salted peanuts, don't show your disapproval. Tell her you like fat mothers.

Fourth: Encourage your parents to talk about their problems. Try to keep in mind that to them things like earning a living and paying off the mortgage are important.

Fifth: Be tolerant of their appearance. When you dad gets a haircut, don't feel personally humiliated. Remember, it's important to him to look like his peers.

Sixth: Most important of all, if they do something you consider wrong, let them know it's their behavior you dislike, not them. Remember, parents need to feel that they are loved.

Some of these are humorous, but I feel they make a needed point. It is a mutual responsibility of both parent and child to make a family a success.

I realize that young people are tempted, when a request is refused, or some requirement is made of them by their parents that is not the popular thing to do, to feel their parents are being contrary or hard to get along with, or maybe just mean to them. If a parent is being mean, he doesn't deserve the honor and respect the Bible requires of the child. But, most parents are simply trying to give their children the guidance, direction and purpose for their lives that they see as the best way, the Bible way. It is from a heart filled with love and concern that these restrictions come.

Such parents deserve your honor and respect! I encourage you, as a young person, to give it! When a parent has your well-being at heart, their advice and help can be some of the best advice you will ever receive. They may make mistakes in judgment, but your good is their goal.

I am thankful for my mother's advice, teaching, and attitudes about life. It has been a blessing to me.

Questions

1. Is there a communication gap between you and your children? What can be done to close that gap and restore good communication?

2. As a young adult, what do I owe my parents after I have left home? Does my responsibility for my parents increase as they grow older?

3. How do I "reap what I sow" in the lives of my children? Can I change the results of my sowing, so the reaping will be different?

4. What suggestions would you give to young people about how they can have a good relationship with their parents?

---

[1]Philip E. Morrison, **Sermons For The Seventies,** Wichita Falls, Texas: Western Christian Foundation.

CHAPTER 14
Creative Discipline

To watch a life unfold, to be directly and intimately involved as a guide to maturity and a supervisor of growth, is what makes being a parent one of the most exciting and rewarding experiences in the world.

Daniel Webster said, "If we work upon marble, it will perish; if we work upon brass, time will efface it; if we rear temples, they will crumble into dust; but if we work upon immortal souls, if we imbue them with principles, with the just fear of the creator and love of fellowman, we engrave on those tables something which will brighten all eternity."

Parents Dream Dreams

You can't be a parent without dreaming dreams. In your arms you hold the future with all its hopes, expectations and possibilities. What are your dreams for your children?

I am not suggesting that you live your life over again through your children, but as a parent you can help your children grow to maturity as a healthy, responsible and loving person.

Also, I realize sometimes people fail, even though they are doing all they know how to do to succeed. I feel it is important for parents to acknowledge their mistakes. "Yes I failed, not because God's word is not true, but because I did not practice it the way I should."

Some have the tendency to say when they fail, "I did it the way God told me too, sometimes it works, and sometimes it doesn't." THAT IS NOT TRUE! When we follow the principles of God's word we always succeed. The failure comes when we are not consistent with what God has said.

But what about the good Christian whose son or daughter turns out to be disrespectful or disruptive? Or, the non-Christian who has a son or daughter who turns out to be a very dedicated Christian?

I realize the child has a responsibility in the matter. Children make the wrong choices. They are responsible for their own choices and their rebellion. But consider the family life of these two families, and you will see why the children rebelled or copied the good they see in their parents.

The non-Christian parents, in my experience, are parents who have certain Christian qualities in their relationship with their children that are often lacking in the Christian home. These qualities help the children see the good and they follow it, or as in the case of the Christian family, see their hypocrisy and rebel against it.

Qualities like the open display of affection of the father for his son. Instead of the cold, negative discipline that often Christian parents think is what the Bible teaches. These are the qualities lacking in the Christian home.

Another quality may be the attitude of training the child, counseling the child, instead of preaching to the child. The popular song entitled, "Papa Don't Preach," says a lot about many Christian parents.

The Christian parent says, "I told them what to do, but they rejected my advice." But discipline is not TELLING them what to do. It is open discussion with your child, where the child feels free to tell you about anything that is worrying him or upsetting him. It is taking the time to instruct him, in love, by words and the example you set by your own life.

I do want to emphasize that neither parent nor child is perfect. As the child grows older he becomes more and more responsible for his own actions and decisions. The parent must let the child know, "I love you no matter what you do."

I think of King David as he raised his children. The Lord promised him, "My faithfulness and My mercy shall be with him." The Lord promised him He would always be faithful to His promises no matter what his children did.

"If his sons forsake My law
and do not walk in my judgments,
If they break my statutes
And do not keep My commandments,
Then I will visit their transgression
with the rod,
And their iniquity with stripes.
Nevertheless My lovingkindness I will
not utterly take from him,
Nor allow My faithfulness to fail.

115

My covenant I will not break,
Nor alter the word that has gone out
of My lips. " Psalm 89:30-34.

God loves us even if we fail. God loves our children, and will continue to love them even if they rebel against Him. He asks us to simply love Him back.

God's principles do work. The problem is our inconsistence in following the principles He has given us.

The Goal Of Discipline

The word **discipline** comes from the root word, "disciple." Normally we think of discipline as punishment. But as you can see from the greek root word, discipline is much, much more.

It means to TEACH and to TRAIN our children in self-discipline, and responsible behavior about life. They need assistance in learning how to face the challenges and obligations of life. They must learn the art of self-control or self-discipline. They must be equipped with the personal strength needed to meet the demands and challenges imposed on them by school, peer groups, and later adult responsibilities.

Good discipline begins with a loving, accepting environment. It begins when a parent plays, feeds, reads, walks, and talks with his child. It means listening and responding patiently to the child because the child is a learner, he is a disciple of the parent.

The Bible gives us a good understanding of the word "discipline" and how it is done.

"My son, do not despise the chastening of the Lord,
Nor detest His correction;
For whom the Lord loves He corrects,
Just as a father the son in whom he delights. "

Proverbs 3:11,12.

To paraphrase what Solomon said, "I should not despise the correction of God. He does this correcting in my daily life. He does this because He loves me. The correcting comes through trials and temptations. Of course, God doesn't send the trials, but He uses them for our growth." (James 1:2-4; 13-17).

"He who spares his rod hates his son, But he who loves him disciplines him promptly. " Proverbs 13:24.

The father that does not discipline his son, that includes spanking when necessary, hates his son. When does he start? Early, "O" years old. I believe that as the child reaches adolescence that the parent needs to be careful about the use of the rod. Sometimes an incorrect

116

use can build resentment, but when it is done in love, the child will see that love and know it is for his best interest.

"Foolishness is bound up in the heart of a child, But the rod of correction will drive it far from him." Proverbs 22:15.

Children do foolish things, but correct discipline will help them know what is right and what is wrong behavior. As a result, they will become responsible adults.

"Do not withhold correction from a child.
For if you beat him with a rod, he will not die.
You shall beat him with a rod,
And deliver his soul from hell." Proverbs 23:13,14.

Don't withhold discipline from your child. Discipline will not kill him. Of course, he is talking about the proper kind of physical punishment. Abuse can kill a child. But proper discipline will keep his soul out of hell. I know from my own experience.

"The rod and reproof give wisdom, But a child left to himself brings shame to his mother." Proverbs 29:15.

Discipline helps the child gain wisdom. When a child is left to find his own way and set his own values he will bring his parents a lot of grief.

"Correct your son, and he will give you rest; Yes, he will give delight to your soul." Proverbs 29:17.

Discipline your child, give him instruction and guidance in his life. When you do, you can have confidence that he will make the right choices and do his best to serve God and be an asset to society. When you know this, you can rest at night. You can be proud of the loving relationship you have with your children.

What benefits are described by Solomon in the above verses for the parent that disciplines his children:

1. You will have peace.
2. You will have the joy in your heart about your children's accomplishments.
3. You will know that your children have wisdom.
4. You will know that your children are responsible people and can choose the correct pathway to God.

What benefits are described by Solomon in the above verses for the child whose parents disciplined him:

1. He knows that his parents love him. They tried to show him the best way of life.
2. He becomes a responsible person and doesn't try to blame others for the mistakes he makes.

3. He gains wisdom by listening to his parent's and other teacher's advice.

4. He will save his soul.

In the New Testament, Paul, the apostle, gives some more instruction:

> *"Fathers, do not provoke your children to wrath, but bring them up in the training and admonition of the Lord."*
> Ephesians 6:4.

Paul says to the father, the spiritual leader of the family, you are not to build resentment in your children by your discipline. Instead, your discipline is to counsel and train that child to love God and his earthly parents. What a fearful responsibility Paul gives to the father.

Principles For Good Discipline

Let me suggest some principles for good and effective discipline. These principles are not hard, fast laws. I don't believe that anyone can lay down rules that will apply to every situation. I have not mastered the art of disciplining my children. I believe both parent and child go through stages of learning as the discipline takes place.

1. The child should understand WHAT the discipline is for and WHY it is being given.[1]

If the child doesn't understand WHY, how can you expect improvement in his behavior as a result of the discipline? "Because I said so!" is blind submission that accomplishes nothing except obedience. When the child understands that what he did was unacceptable behavior, and why, then he has a solid basis for choosing the proper behavior next time.

2. The discipline should be fair. The child should get some idea of how serious the offense is by the severity of the discipline imposed.

A child learns to judge behavior by the kind of parental response it brings. So, only through fair discipline can he get an accurate view of the way his good or bad behavior fits into the world, or in our society.

For example, parents should not take away a summer camping trip for some minor offense, nor should they punish a major offense by some gentle reminder. If your teenager is caught drinking beer, or lying, just saying "Honey don't do that anymore," is not fair punishment. Serious offenses deserve serious punishments.

3. Discipline should be consistent. A parent's response to his child's behavior sometimes depends on little more than what kind of day the parent has had. This type of discipline is wrong and unfair to the child.

It is unfair to the child because it robs him of an opportunity to see

118

his own behavior in a clear light. What is unacceptable today may be all right tomorrow. That type of inconsistence only confuses the child. So the parent is responsible for consistence in his discipline. He needs to show the same level of approval or disapproval for each offense.

I realize absolute consistence is impossible to achieve, but the closer you get, the more help you will provide your child.

4. Discipline should be as closely related to the offense as possible.

If a child makes a mess, the child should be responsible for cleaning up the mess. Don't do it for him. Small children can help you. Take the time for them to learn. If you do it for them, they learn that mom and dad will clean it up for me.

If a child leaves a tool out of place after he uses it, he should be made to return it or denied use of it for a period of time.

If a child is late returning from playing with a friend, or date, don't allow him to go to that friend's house, or go on a date for a period of time.

You be the judge as to the amount of punishment that is appropriate.

5. The discipline chosen must not harm the child. Discipline that breaks bones, or cuts the skin, or burns, or bruises the skin, even if they were used by your parents, are **not acceptable measures of discipline.** God is not pleased when a parent abuses his child.

Also, I want to add, that measures of discipline that harm the child emotionally, as being locked in a closet, or called stupid, or dummy, or any other thing, are **unacceptable forms of discipline.** We don't have to humiliate a child to discipline him!

Any measure that is brutal, or harsh, or degrading will do more harm to that child than good. Perhaps it will inflict some permanent damage to the child. As parents we want good for our children, not harm. Build their self-esteem, don't tear it down!

6. Discipline should be administered by someone who loves the child and is loved by the child.

A stranger cannot appropriately discipline my child. Nor can I effectively discipline someone else's child that I do not know or love. It is in the context of love, support, encouragement, acceptance and affirmation that discipline will accomplish what it is designed to do. It says, "I love you, I want you to be a better person and happy about life and I know you can't achieve that if you continue to follow your present course."

Let me suggest one method of discipline that children and parents can enjoy and grow closer to each other by doing. It is called, "Family Night." It is a night in the week, when the family sets aside two or

119

three hours for an activity and/or Bible study and discussion.

You may have to unplug your phone, and lock the doors, but take this time especially for play and talking with each other as a family. Don't let anything interfere with this special time.

It may be an outing together at some recreational park, or a trip to the beach. Anything that lets you enjoy your time together and allows communication.

Also, allow for Bible study and discussion of God's word in an open fashion with your spouse and children. Sometimes the questions are hard to answer; sometimes you may have to say, "I don't know;" sometimes you may have to say, "I'm sorry for what I did;" sometimes you may cry together; sometimes you will discover something you did not know. But, every session will be a blessing for you and your family and will draw you closer to each other.

I know that my wife and my children know me better, and I know them better because of times like "Family Night."

This type of teaching and training, which is real discipline, will make your family life GREAT! Your children will love God and know how to use the word of God to help them live joyfully in a world of sin. Try it!

Questions

1. What dreams do you have for your children? What are you doing to help them achieve those dreams?

2. How do you encourage your children? Do you preach to them; nag at them; talk to them; sit down and have a discussion; allow them to say whatever they feel like saying; etc.?

3. How would you define discipline? Do you feel that the discipline you practice with your children is fair, or unfair? Why?

4. Do your children describe you as a understanding parent and one they enjoy being with, or as some one they can't talk to? What are their reasons and do you understand why they feel that way?

5. What suggestions for discipline would you add to the list?

---

[1]Carl Brecheen, **What Every Family Needs,** (Austin, Texas:) Sweet Publishing Co., 1979.

Bibliography

Brecheen, Carl and Faulkner, Paul. **What Every Family Needs.** Austin, Texas: Sweet Publishing Company, 1979.

Bryan, Alan. **Climbing Happiness Mountain.** Florence, Alabama: Success Dynamics, Inc., 1978.

Coopersmith, Stanley. "Self-respect In Children." **Scientific American,** February, 1968.

"Counseling Married Couples With Sexual Problems." **Quarterly Newsletter for Christian Family Services.** October, 1986.

Curran, Delores. **Traits Of A Healthy Family.** Minneapolis, Minnesota: Winston Press, 1983.

Dodson, James. **What Wives Wish Their Husbands Knew About Women.** Wheaton, Illinois: Tyndale Press, 1975.

Handford, Elizabeth Rice. **Me? Obey Him?** Murfreesboro, Tennessee: Sword Of The Lord Publishers, 1972.

Hazelip, Harold. "Traits of a Healthy Family." **UpReach,** January, 1985.

Herald of Truth. Produced by the Highland Church of Christ, Abilene, Texas.

LaHaye, Tim and Beverly. **The Act of Marriage.** Grand Rapids, Michigan: Zondervan, 1976.

Levin, Robert and Amy. "Sexual Pleasure: The Surprising Preferences in 100,000 Women." **Redbook,** September, 1975.

Mace, David. "Marriage As Relationship-in Depth." Edited by H.L. Silverman. **Marital Therapy.** Springfield, Illinois: Thomas, 1972.

Maltz, Maxwell. **Psycho-Cybernetics.** New York: Essandess.

McKnight, Mid. **Vestibules Of Heaven.** Abilene, Texas: McKnight Publications.

Menninger, Karl. **Love Against Hate.** New York: Harcourt, Bruce, and World, 1942. (A Harvest Book).

Men's Manual. Oak Brook, Illinois: Institute In Basic Youth Conflicts, Inc.

Powell, John. **Why Am I Afraid To Tell You Who I Am?** Valencia, California: Tabor Publishing, 1978.

Narramore, Bruce. **You're Somebody Special.** Grand Rapids, Michigan: Zondervan, 1978.

Powell, John. **Why Am I Afraid To Tell You Who I Am?** Niles, Illinois: Argus Communications, 1969.

Rogers, Clifton. "The Happy Christian Home." A paper presented at the Harding University Lectureships, 1969.

Smalley, Gary. **If Only He Knew.** Grand Rapids, Michigan: Zondervan, 1979.

Stevenson, Dwight. **Faith Takes A Name.** New York: Harper, 1954.

Wheat, Ed. **Love Life For Every Married Couple.** Springdale, Arkansas: Bible Believers Publishers.

_____ . "Sex Problems and Sex Technique In Marriage." Springdale, Arkansas: Bible Believers Publishers.

Wright, Norman. **Communication, Key To Your Marriage.** Ventura, California: Gospel Light Publications.

Other Books From Quality Publications

ADULT

At The Master's Feet *by J. J. Turner*
Build Your Bible Knowledge - Acts *by John Hudson Tiner*
Commentary On Ephesians *by Benny B. Bristow*
From Burden To Joy *by Bill Boverie*
If I Had One More Sermon To Preach *by Edward P. Myers*
Modern Messages From The Minor Prophets *by David Pharr*
Moments With The Master *by Stephen D. Boyd*
Step Out Of The Crowd *by J. J. Turner*
Studies In The Book Of Daniel *by Leslie G. Thomas*
Studies In Colossians *by John L. Kachelman, Jr.*

LADIES

Be Still And Know That I Am God *by Wanda Jo Pence*
Does God Delight In Me? *by Betty Nowlin Edwards*
The Hand Of God Touched Me *by Stella Gatewood-Wester*
Leaves Only *by Jo Ann Mills*
A New Song *by Alice Ivy Cravens*
Speaking To You Of Grief *by Martha Oliver Williams*
Quality Cooking *(Cookbook) Compilation*

YOUTH

Be King Of The Mountain *by Ralph G. Bryant*
Called To Be Champions *by J. J. Turner*
Highway To Heaven *by Barry Cunningham*

CHILDREN

Because God Loves Us *by Susan Bachman*

These and other books are available from your local bookstore or from Quality Publications, P.O. Box 1060, Abilene, Texas 79604, (915) 677-6262.